Manual for the
YOUTH
SELF-REPORT

and
1991 PROFILE

Thomas M. Achenbach
Department of Psychiatry
University of Vermont

NOTE: Windows software is available for the YSR and other instruments of the Achenbach System of Empirically Based Assessment (ASEBA).

All ASEBA materials can be ordered from:
ASEBA
1 South Prospect St.
Burlington, VT 05401-3456
Web: http://Checklist.uvm.edu   Fax: 802/656-2602

Proper bibliographic citation for this *Manual*:
Achenbach, T.M. (1991). *Manual for the Youth Self-Report and 1991 Profile*. Burlington, VT: University of Vermont Department of Psychiatry.

Related Books

Achenbach, T.M. (1991). *Integrative guide for the 1991 CBCL/4-18, YSR, and TRF profiles*. Burlington, VT: University of Vermont Department of Psychiatry.

Achenbach, T.M. (1991). *Manual for the Child Behavior Checklist/4-18 and 1991 Profile*. Burlington, VT: University of Vermont Department of Psychiatry.

Achenbach, T.M. (1991). *Manual for the Teacher's Report Form and 1991 Profile*. Burlington, VT: University of Vermont Department of Psychiatry.

Achenbach, T.M. (1993). *Empirically based taxonomy: How to use syndromes and profile types derived from the CBCL/4-18, TRF, and YSR*. Burlington, VT: University of Vermont Department of Psychiatry.

Achenbach, T.M. (1997). *Manual for the Young Adult Self-Report and Young Adult Behavior Checklist*. Burlington, VT: University of Vermont Department of Psychiatry.

Achenbach, T.M., & McConaughy, S.H. (1997). *Empirically based assessment of child and adolescent psychopathology. Practical applications*. (2nd ed). Thousand Oaks, CA: Sage.

Library of Congress #90-72109   ISBN 0-938565-09-5
Printed in the United States of America 12 11 10 9 8

USER QUALIFICATIONS

The Youth Self-Report (YSR) is designed to be filled out by youths who are 11 to 18 years old. It can also be administered orally to those who have poor reading skills, as described in Chapter 1. Although the YSR is intended to be self-explanatory for youths having at least fifth grade reading skills, users should introduce the YSR in a tactful and sensitive manner appropriate for the situation. In most situations, an appropriate introduction would be: "We would like you to fill out this form in order to obtain your views of your interests, feelings, and behavior." The youth should be assured of confidentiality, which should be strictly guarded.

After the YSR is introduced, an adult who is familiar with the YSR should remain available to answer any questions. Questions should be answered in a factual and objective manner to help the youth understand the literal meaning of items, rather than to probe his or her thoughts.

When the YSR has been completed, it can be used as a take-off point for clinical interviewing. The interviewer can ask if the youth would like to discuss any of the items and can ask for further information on issues raised by the YSR responses. Using the YSR in this fashion requires training and experience in interviewing adolescents. For many adolescents, the YSR is an effective "ice breaker" that stimulates them to talk about their concerns. Clinical use of the YSR requires skills commensurate with at least the Master's degree level in psychology, social work, or special education, or two years of residency in psychiatry.

The YSR should be scored on the scales appropriate for the respondent's sex. It is also important to compare the results with data from other sources, such as parents, teachers, observations, interviews, tests, and biomedical assessment. The user must therefore have access to multiple sources of information about the respondent and must be trained in the theory and methodology of standardized assessment, as well as in work with adolescents. No amount of prior training, however, can substitute for professional maturity and a thorough knowledge of the procedures and cautions presented in this *Manual*.

All users should understand that the YSR is designed to obtain self-reports of feelings and behavior in a standardized fashion for comparison with reports by normative groups of 11- to 18-year-olds. No item or score should be automatically equated with any particular diagnosis or inferred disorder. Instead, the responsible professional will integrate self-report data with other types of data in the comprehensive evaluation of adolescents and their families.

PREFACE

The pre-1991 profiles for scoring the YSR, CBCL, and TRF were developed separately as data were accumulated for each one. The syndrome scales of each profile were designed to capture the patterns of problems specifically identified for each sex within particular age ranges on each instrument taken separately.

The pre-1991 syndrome scales functioned well for describing and assessing patterns that were empirically derived for specific sex/age groups as seen by a particular type of informant. The 1991 editions are designed to advance both the conceptual structure and the practical applications of empirically based assessment by focusing more precisely on the syndromes that are common to both sexes and different age ranges, according to parent-, self-, and teacher-reports.

The 1991 profiles for scoring data from all three sources include a common set of eight syndromes that are normed on the same national sample. However, to reflect important sex and age differences, the syndromes are normed separately for each sex within particular age ranges, according to reports by each type of informant. In addition, items found to be associated with a syndrome in ratings by a particular type of informant are retained for scoring by that type of informant. Some additional syndromes and competence scales are also specific to particular sex/age groups as seen by a particular kind of informant. For example, a syndrome designated as Self-Destructive/Identity Problems was found in boys' self-ratings but was not found in girls self-ratings nor in parent- or teacher-ratings. This syndrome is therefore scored only from boys' YSR ratings.

Although this *Manual* was written by a single author, the first person plural "we" is used throughout. This reflects the author's feeling that the work is a joint product of many coworkers, especially the following: Neil Aguiar, Janet Arnold, Jill Brown, Bruce Compas, Craig Edelbrock, Judy Ewell, Catherine Howell, Lynda Howell, David Jacobowitz, Stephanie McConaughy, Susan Oakes, Vicky Phares, Michael Sawyer, Catherine Stanger, Gavin Stewart, Frank Verhulst, and John Weisz. I deeply appreciate the contributions of all these people, plus the many others who have contributed through their own work and comments.

Much of the work reported here has been supported by University Associates in Psychiatry, a nonprofit health services and research corporation of the University of Vermont Department of Psychiatry. I am also grateful for the Spencer Foundation's support of our recent research on teachers' reports and for the National Institute of Mental Health's support of research that has contributed to this effort.

The Reader's Guide below offers an overview of the contents to aid users in quickly locating the material they seek.

READER'S GUIDE

I. **Introductory Material Needed by Most Readers**

    A. Description of the YSR
    and Multiaxial Assessment .... Chapter 1
    B. Competence Scales Scored from the YSR .... Chapter 2
    C. Problem Scales Scored from the YSR .... Chapter 3
    D. Internalizing and Externalizing
    Groupings of Syndromes .... Chapter 4

II. **Statistical Data on Reliability and Validity**

    A. Reliability and Stability .... Chapter 5
    B. Validity .... Chapter 6
    C. Item Scores .... Chapter 7

III. **Relations Between the Pre-1991
and 1991 Scales** .... Chapter 8

IV. **Applications of the YSR and Profile**

    A. Practical Applications .... Chapter 9
    B. Research Use .... Chapter 10

  V. **Instruments Related to the YSR** .... Chapter 11

 VI. **Answers to Commonly Asked Questions** .... Chapter 12

VII. **Instructions for Hand Scoring
the Profile** .... Appendix A

VIII. **Mean Scale Scores for Matched Referred
and Nonreferred Samples** .... Appendix B

 IX. **Correlations Among Scales** .... Appendix C

CONTENTS

User Qualifications iii
Preface iv
Reader's Guide v

1. The Youth Self-Report 1
Multiaxial Empirically Based Assessment 2
Competence Items of the YSR 5
Problem Items of the YSR 8
Administration of the YSR 11
Summary 12

2. Competence Scales 14
Norming the Competence Scales 16
Assignment of Percentiles and *T* Scores to Competence Scales 18
    Activities and Social Scale Scores 18
    Total Competence Score 23
Summary 24

3. Syndrome and Total Problem Scales 25
Pre-1991 Syndromes 26
Derivation of the 1991 Syndromes 27
    Principal Components Analyses 28
    Rotations of Principal Components 28
    Derivation of Core Syndromes 30
    Cross-Informant Syndromes 32
Profiles for Scoring the 1991 Syndromes 34
Assigning Normalized *T* Scores to Syndrome Scales 38
    Lowest *T* Scores 38
    Highest *T* Scores 40
Assigning Normalized *T* Scores to Total Problem Scores 41
Normal, Borderline, and Clinical Ranges 43
    Syndrome Scales 43
    Total Problem Score 45
Summary 46

4. Internalizing and Externalizing Groupings of Syndromes 47
1991 Internalizing and Externalizing Groupings 48
Assignment of Internalizing and Externalizing *T* Scores 50
Relations Between Internalizing and Externalizing Scores 51
    Distinguishing Between Internalizing and Externalizing Patterns . 52
Summary 53

5. **Test-Retest Reliability and Stability** 55
   Longer-Term Stability of YSR Scales 58
   Internal Consistency 59
   Summary 60

6. **Validity** 62
   Content Validity of YSR Items 63
   Criterion-Related Validity of YSR Scales 65
      Referral Status Differences Between Scale Scores 66
      Demographic Differences Between Scale Scores 68
   Classification of Youths According To Clinical Cutpoints 72
      Odds Ratios 73
      Combined Competence and Problem Scores 76
      Discriminant Analyses 77
   Probability of Particular Total Scores Being from the Referred Versus
      Nonreferred Samples 80
   Summary 81

7. **Item Scores** 83
   Competence Items 83
      Referral Status Differences in Competence Scores 84
      Demographic Differences in Competence Scores 86
   Problem Item Scores 90
      Referral Status Differences in Problem Scores 91
      Demographic Differences in Problem Scores 97
   Summary 120

8. **Relations Between Pre-1991 and 1991 YSR Scales** 122
   Construction of Scales 123
      Syndrome Scales 123
      Internalizing and Externalizing 126
      Total Problem Score 127
   Statistical Relations Between Pre-1991 and 1991 Scales 127
   Summary 128

9. **Practical Applications of the YSR and Profile** 130
   Applications in Mental Health Contexts 132
      Intake and Evaluation 132
      Clinical Interviewing 133
      Planning Interventions 134
      Reassessments During and After Intervention 136
      Case Example 137
   Applications in School Contexts 144
      Case Example 148
      Confidentiality in School Settings 150

Applications in Medical Contexts 151
Forensic Applications 153
Diagnostic Issues 154
Planning and Accountability for Services 155
    Needs Assessment 157
    Accountability for Services 157
    Case Registers 159
Training of Practitioners 159
    Training for Intake Assessments 160
    Selecting Teaching Cases 160
    Comparing Data from Different Sources 160
Summary 161

10. **Research Use of the YSR and Profile** 163
Use of Raw Scores Versus *T* Scores in Research with the YSR 165
    Statistical Analysis of Scale Scores 166
Research Including Both Sexes 167
Epidemiological Research 169
    Population Studies 170
    Case Registers 171
Diagnostic and Taxonomic Research 172
Etiological Research 174
Outcome Research 176
    Groups at Risk 177
Experimental Intervention Studies 177
Studies of Diagnostic Constructs 178
Abused Youths 179
Research on Medical Conditions 180
Cross-Cultural Research 182
Summary 184

11. **Assessment Materials Related to the YSR** 185
Young Adult Self-Report 189
Summary 190

12. **Answers to Commonly Asked Questions** 191
Questions About the YSR 191
Scoring the YSR 196
The YSR Profile 200

References 205

Appendix

A. Instructions for Hand Scoring
   the Youth Self-Report 210

B. Mean Scale Scores for Matched Referred
   and Nonreferred Samples 215

C. Pearson Correlations Among *T* Scores 217

Index 219

Chapter 1
The Youth Self-Report

This is a revision of the *Manual for the Youth Self-Report and Profile* (Achenbach & Edelbrock, 1987). The current revision is necessitated by changes in the 1991 scoring profile, new national norms, and new provisions for coordinating self-report data with data obtained from parents and teachers.

Some small changes have been made in the wording of the 1991 Youth Self-Report (YSR), but these do not affect scoring. The main change is in YSR problem item *42*, which is now *I would rather be alone than with others*, as compared to the pre-1991 version, *I like to be alone*. Similar changes have been made in the 1991 editions of the Child Behavior Checklist for Ages 4-18 (CBCL/4-18; Achenbach, 1991b) and the Teacher's Report Form (TRF; Achenbach, 1991c), which obtain parents' and teachers' reports in formats similar to that of the YSR. Because the changes are minor, the pre-1991 editions of the YSR, CBCL/4-18, and TRF can be scored on the 1991 versions of their respective profiles. Conversely, the 1991 editions of the YSR, CBCL/4-18, and TRF can be scored on the earlier versions of their profiles. Continuity can thus be maintained in scoring data obtained with the 1991 and pre-1991 editions of the YSR, as well as with its counterpart forms for parent and teacher reports.

To aid readers who are unfamiliar with the YSR, as well as those who are familiar with it, this *Manual* first presents the multiaxial assessment model on which the YSR is based. Thereafter, the YSR itself is described. Chapter 2 presents the scales for scoring the competence items on the 1991 YSR profile, while Chapter 3 presents the scales for scoring the problem items. Internalizing and Externalizing groupings of

1

problem scales are presented in Chapter 4. Chapter 5 deals with the reliability and stability of scores obtained from the YSR. Chapter 6 provides evidence for validity and the basis for scale score cutpoints that distinguish between the normal, borderline, and clinical ranges.

Statistical and graphic comparisons of item scores obtained by referred and nonreferred children are presented in Chapter 7. Chapter 8 presents relations between the 1991 profile and the pre-1991 edition. Applications in practical and research contexts are presented in Chapters 9 and 10, respectively. Chapter 11 provides data on relations to CBCL/4-18 and TRF scores, while Chapter 12 provides answers to commonly asked questions. Instructions for hand scoring the 1991 YSR profile can be found in Appendix A, while psychometric data on the scale scores are displayed in Appendix B and C.

MULTIAXIAL EMPIRICALLY BASED ASSESSMENT

The YSR is designed to obtain 11- to 18-year-olds' reports of their own competencies and problems in a standardized format. It includes many of the same items as the CBCL/4-18 and the TRF. The subjects' knowledge of their own behavior and emotions makes them potentially important contributors to the assessment process. Cognitive and social immaturity limit the ability of young children to recall and report the way they feel and behave across a variety of situations. Adolescents, however, are cognitively better equipped to provide reports of their own feelings and behavior across situations. The YSR was therefore developed to obtain adolescents' views of their own functioning in ways that would facilitate comparison with other assessment procedures, such as the CBCL/4-18 and TRF.

Even though adolescents presumably know their own behavior better than others do, this does not mean that adolescents' self-reports should be the ultimate criterion for accuracy.

What individuals report about themselves is apt to be affected by their recall at the moment, how they construe the questions, their candor, and their self-judgment. Consequently, adolescents' self-reports may be less accurate in some respects than reports by other informants, such as parents or teachers. Adolescents' self-reports are not, therefore, necessarily better than reports by others. Instead, adolescents' self-reports constitute one facet of assessment that should include reports by informants who see the adolescents in different contexts, as well as by the adolescents themselves.

Although the YSR can be used alone to obtain adolescents' reports of their own competencies and problems, users should recognize that no single source of data provides a complete picture of adolescents' functioning. The YSR is therefore viewed as one component of an approach to assessment that employs data from multiple sources, such as parents, teachers, tests, physical assessments, direct observations, and interviews. We call this approach *multiaxial assessment* to emphasize that multiple sources of data should be used.

When discrepancies are found between different sources, this does not necessarily mean that the sources are unreliable, or that one is wrong and another is right, or that one source should take precedence over another. Nor does it mean that all sources should converge on a single diagnostic category. On the contrary, different sources may validly reveal different facets of an adolescent's functioning, each of which deserves attention when evaluating needs for help, planning interventions, and evaluating outcomes.

The *Integrative Guide for the 1991 CBCL/4-18, YSR, and TRF Profiles* (Achenbach, 1991a) presents a model of multiaxial assessment for the preschool years through adolescence. As applied to the assessment of adolescents, the model includes the following five axes:

Axis I—Parent Data. Standardized ratings of the adolescent by parents, as on the CBCL; history of the adolescent's development, problems, competencies, and interests as reported by the parents; interviews with parents; workability of parents for various potential interventions.

Axis II—Teacher Data. Standardized ratings of the adolescent by teachers, such as on the TRF; other teacher data, such as report cards, comments in school records, and interviews with teachers; workability of teachers for various potential interventions.

Axis III—Cognitive Assessment. Ability tests, such as the WISC and WAIS-R; achievement tests; tests of perceptual-motor and speech-language functioning.

Axis IV—Physical Assessment. Height and weight; physical abnormalities and handicaps; medical and neurological examinations.

Axis V—Direct Assessment of the Adolescent. Standardized self-ratings paralleling parent and teacher ratings, as on the YSR; clinical interview; direct observations in customary environments such as school, recorded with instruments such as the Direct Observation Form (DOF, see Achenbach, 1991b); self-concept measures; personality tests; workability for various potential interventions.

Table 1-1 summarizes the components of the multiaxial model in abbreviated form as it applies to the 11- to 18-year age range. The model provides guidelines rather than rigid prescriptions that must be precisely followed in all cases. Additional assessment procedures—such as sociometrics and family assessment—can be added to those listed in Table 1-1, if desired.

Table 1-1
Examples of Multiaxial Assessment of Adolescents

Axis I Parent Reports	Axis II Teacher Reports	Axis III Cognitive Assessment	Axis IV Physical Assessment	Axis V Direct Assessment
CBCL	TRF	WISC WAIS-R	Height	YSR
Developmental history	School records	Achievement perceptual-motor,	Weight	DOF
	Teacher interview		Medical	Interview
Parent interview		speech-language tests	Neuro-logical	Self-concept, personality tests

COMPETENCE ITEMS OF THE YSR

Figure 1-1 shows the competence items that appear on pages 1 and 2 of the YSR. These items generally parallel the competence items of the CBCL/4-18. The rationale and development of the CBCL competence items are presented in the CBCL *Manual* (Achenbach, 1991b). The YSR omits the CBCL questions about special class placement and grade retention, which were deemed inappropriate to ask youths to report about themselves. Accurate information about grade retention and special class placement is more likely to be obtained from parents and teachers anyway. YSR Items I-VII are scored on the competence scales of the profile described in Chapter 2.

Following the competence items, page 2 of the YSR provides open-ended items for youths to describe illnesses, disabilities, concerns about school, other concerns, and the best things about themselves. These items are not designed to be

YOUTH SELF-REPORT FOR AGES 11–18

For office use only
ID #

YOUR NAME

PARENTS' USUAL TYPE OF WORK, even if not working now *(Please be specific — for example, auto mechanic, high school teacher, homemaker, laborer, lathe operator, shoe salesman, army sergeant.)*

YOUR SEX	YOUR AGE	ETHNIC GROUP OR RACE
☐ Boy ☐ Girl		

FATHER'S TYPE OF WORK: _____

TODAY'S DATE   Mo._____ Date_____ Yr._____

YOUR BIRTHDATE   Mo._____ Date_____ Yr._____

MOTHER'S TYPE OF WORK: _____

GRADE IN SCHOOL _____

NOT ATTENDING SCHOOL ☐

IF YOU ARE WORKING, STATE TYPE OF WORK

Please fill out this form to reflect *your* views, even if other people might not agree. Feel free to write additional comments beside each item and in the spaces provided on pages 2 and 4.

I. Please list the sports you most like to take part in. For example: swimming, baseball, skating, skate boarding, bike riding, fishing, etc.

☐ None

Compared to others of your age, about how much time do you spend in each?

Less Than Average	Average	More Than Average

Compared to others of your age, how well do you do each one?

Below Average	Average	Above Average

a._____   ☐ ☐ ☐   ☐ ☐ ☐

b._____   ☐ ☐ ☐   ☐ ☐ ☐

c._____   ☐ ☐ ☐   ☐ ☐ ☐

II. Please list your favorite hobbies, activities, and games, other than sports. For example: cards, books, piano, autos, crafts, etc. (Do **not** include listening to radio or TV.)

☐ None

Compared to others of your age, about how much time do you spend in each?

Less Than Average	Average	More Than Average

Compared to others of your age, how well do you do each one?

Below Average	Average	Above Average

a._____   ☐ ☐ ☐   ☐ ☐ ☐

b._____   ☐ ☐ ☐   ☐ ☐ ☐

c._____   ☐ ☐ ☐   ☐ ☐ ☐

III. Please list any organizations, clubs, teams or groups you belong to.

☐ None

Compared to others of your age, how active are you in each?

Less Active	Average	More Active

a._____   ☐ ☐ ☐

b._____   ☐ ☐ ☐

c._____   ☐ ☐ ☐

IV. Please list any jobs or chores you have. For example: Paper route, babysitting, making bed, working in store, etc. (Include **both** paid and unpaid jobs and chores.)

☐ None

Compared to others of your age, how well do you carry them out?

Below Average	Average	Above Average

a._____   ☐ ☐ ☐

b._____   ☐ ☐ ☐

c._____   ☐ ☐ ☐

Figure 1-1. Competence Items I-IV of the YSR.

V.   **1. About how many close friends do you have?**   ☐ None   ☐ 1   ☐ 2 or 3   ☐ 4 or more
(Do not include brothers & sisters)

2. About how many times a week do you do things with any friends outside of regular school hours?
(Do not include brothers & sisters)   ☐ less than 1   ☐ 1 or 2   ☐ 3 or more

VI.   **Compared to others of your age, how well do you:**

	Worse	About the same	Better	
a. Get along with your brothers & sisters?	☐	☐	☐	☐ I have no brothers or sisters
b. Get along with other kids?	☐	☐	☐	
c. Get along with your parents?	☐	☐	☐	
d. Do things by yourself?	☐	☐	☐	

VII.   **Performance in academic subjects.**   ☐ I do not go to school because _____

	Failing	Below Average	Average	Above Average
a. English or Language Arts	☐	☐	☐	☐
b. History or Social Studies	☐	☐	☐	☐
c. Arithmetic or Math	☐	☐	☐	☐
d. Science	☐	☐	☐	☐
Other academic subjects — for example: computer courses, foreign language, business. Do *not* include gym, shop, driver's ed., etc. e. _____	☐	☐	☐	☐
f. _____	☐	☐	☐	☐
g. _____	☐	☐	☐	☐

Do you have any illness, physical disability, or handicap?   ☐ No   ☐ Yes — please describe

Please describe any concerns or problems you have about school:

Please describe any other concerns you have:

Please describe the best things about yourself:

Figure 1-1 (cont.) Competence Items V-VII of the YSR.

scored but to yield useful background information and starting points for interviews.

PROBLEM ITEMS OF THE YSR

As shown in Figure 1-2, pages 3 and 4 of the YSR list problem items to which the youth responds by circling *0* if the item is *not true*; *1* if the item is *somewhat or sometimes true*; and *2* if the item is *very true or often true*. The problem items are similar to those of the CBCL/4-18, except for minor differences in wording and the substitution of 16 socially desirable items that replace problem items which were deemed inappropriate to ask adolescents, mostly because the problems are characteristic of younger ages. (The CBCL *Manual* presents the rationale for the problem list and the 3-step response scale.) The 16 socially desirable items are marked with superscript *a* in Figure 1-2. They are not scored on the problem portion of the profile, which is presented in Chapter 3.

Note that the items shown in Figure 1-2 are numbered 1-112, but that Item 56 includes physical problems a-g, plus the open-ended item 56h for entering additional physical problems, for a total of 119 items. Because 16 of the items are socially desirable characteristics, the total number of specific problem items is 102, plus the open-ended item 56h. Items *2. I have an allergy* and *4. I have asthma* are not counted toward the 1991 total problem score, because they did not discriminate significantly between clinically referred and nonreferred samples in either the YSR or CBCL/4-18. If a youth circled *2* for the remaining 100 specific problem items and *2* for an additional physical problem listed by the youth in Item 56h, the total problem score would be 101 x 2 = 202.

As shown in Figure 1-2, space is provided at the bottom of page 4 to "write down anything else that describes your feelings, behavior, or interests." The responses are useful in

Below is a list of items that describe kids. For each item that describes you **now** or **within the past 6 months**, please circle the **2** if the item is **very true** or **often true** of you. Circle the **1** if the item is **somewhat** or **sometimes true** of you. If the item is **not true** of you, circle the **0**.

0 = Not True   1 = Somewhat or Sometimes True   2 = Very True or Often True

0 1 2	1. I act too young for my age
0 1 2	2. I have an allergy (describe): _____
0 1 2	3. I argue a lot
0 1 2	4. I have asthma
0 1 2	a 5. I act like the opposite sex
0 1 2	6. I like animals
0 1 2	7. I brag
0 1 2	8. I have trouble concentrating or paying attention
0 1 2	9. I can't get my mind off certain thoughts (describe): _____
0 1 2	10. I have trouble sitting still
0 1 2	11. I'm too dependent on adults
0 1 2	12. I feel lonely
0 1 2	13. I feel confused or in a fog
0 1 2	a 14. I cry a lot
0 1 2	15. I am pretty honest
0 1 2	16. I am mean to others
0 1 2	17. I daydream a lot
0 1 2	18. I deliberately try to hurt or kill myself
0 1 2	19. I try to get a lot of attention
0 1 2	20. I destroy my own things
0 1 2	21. I destroy things belonging to others
0 1 2	22. I disobey my parents
0 1 2	23. I disobey at school
0 1 2	24. I don't eat as well as I should
0 1 2	25. I don't get along with other kids
0 1 2	26. I don't feel guilty after doing something I shouldn't
0 1 2	a 27. I am jealous of others
0 1 2	28. I am willing to help others when they need help
0 1 2	29. I am afraid of certain animals, situations, or places, other than school (describe): _____
0 1 2	30. I am afraid of going to school
0 1 2	31. I am afraid I might think or do something bad
0 1 2	32. I feel that I have to be perfect
0 1 2	33. I feel that no one loves me
0 1 2	34. I feel that others are out to get me
0 1 2	35. I feel worthless or inferior
0 1 2	36. I accidentally get hurt a lot
0 1 2	37. I get in many fights
0 1 2	38. I get teased a lot
0 1 2	39. I hang around with kids who get in trouble

0 1 2	40. I hear sounds or voices that other people think aren't there (describe): _____
0 1 2	41. I act without stopping to think
0 1 2	42. I would rather be alone than with others
0 1 2	43. I lie or cheat
0 1 2	44. I bite my fingernails
0 1 2	45. I am nervous or tense
0 1 2	46. Parts of my body twitch or make nervous movements (describe): _____
0 1 2	47. I have nightmares
0 1 2	48. I am not liked by other kids
0 1 2	a 49. I can do certain things better than most kids
0 1 2	50. I am too fearful or anxious
0 1 2	51. I feel dizzy
0 1 2	52. I feel too guilty
0 1 2	53. I eat too much
0 1 2	54. I feel overtired
0 1 2	55. I am overweight
	56. Physical problems without known medical cause:
0 1 2	a. Aches or pains (**not** headaches)
0 1 2	b. Headaches
0 1 2	c. Nausea, feel sick
0 1 2	d. Problems with eyes (describe): _____
0 1 2	e. Rashes or other skin problems
0 1 2	f. Stomachaches or cramps
0 1 2	g. Vomiting, throwing up
0 1 2	h. Other (describe): _____
0 1 2	57. I physically attack people
0 1 2	58. I pick my skin or other parts of my body (describe): _____
0 1 2	a 59. I can be pretty friendly
0 1 2	a 60. I like to try new things
0 1 2	61. My school work is poor
0 1 2	62. I am poorly coordinated or clumsy
0 1 2	63. I would rather be with older kids than with kids my own age

Please see other side

Figure 1-2. Problem and socially desirable Items 1-63 of the YSR. Superscript *a* indicates socially desirable items.

0 = Not True   1 = Somewhat or Sometimes True   2 = Very True or Often True

0 1 2	64. I would rather be with younger kids than with kids my own age
0 1 2	65. I refuse to talk
0 1 2	66. I repeat certain actions over and over (describe): _____
	_____
	_____
0 1 2	67. I run away from home
0 1 2	68. I scream a lot
0 1 2	69. I am secretive or keep things to myself
0 1 2	70. I see things that other people think aren't there (describe):_____
	_____
	_____
0 1 2	71. I am self-conscious or easily embarrassed
0 1 2	72. I set fires
0 1 2	^{a}73. I can work well with my hands
0 1 2	74. I show off or clown
0 1 2	75. I am shy
0 1 2	76. I sleep less than most kids
0 1 2	77. I sleep more than most kids during day and/or night (describe): _____
	_____
	_____
0 1 2	^{a}78. I have a good imagination
0 1 2	79. I have a speech problem (describe): _____
	_____
	_____
0 1 2	^{a}80. I stand up for my rights
0 1 2	81. I steal at home
0 1 2	82. I steal from places other than home
0 1 2	83. I store up things I don't need (describe):
	_____
	_____
0 1 2	84. I do things other people think are strange (describe): _____
	_____
	_____

0 1 2	85. I have thoughts that other people would think are strange (describe): _____
	_____
	_____
	_____
	_____
0 1 2	86. I am stubborn
0 1 2	87. My moods or feelings change suddenly
0 1 2	^{a}88. I enjoy being with other people
0 1 2	89. I am suspicious
0 1 2	90. I swear or use dirty language
0 1 2	91. I think about killing myself
0 1 2	^{a}92. I like to make others laugh
0 1 2	93. I talk too much
0 1 2	94. I tease others a lot
0 1 2	95. I have a hot temper
0 1 2	96. I think about sex too much
0 1 2	97. I threaten to hurt people
0 1 2	^{a}98. I like to help others
0 1 2	99. I am too concerned about being neat or clean
0 1 2	100. I have trouble sleeping (describe): _____
	_____
	_____
0 1 2	101. I cut classes or skip school
0 1 2	102. I don't have much energy
0 1 2	103. I am unhappy, sad, or depressed
0 1 2	104. I am louder than other kids
0 1 2	105. I use alcohol or drugs for nonmedical purposes (describe): _____
	_____
	_____
0 1 2	^{a}106. I try to be fair to others
0 1 2	^{a}107. I enjoy a good joke
0 1 2	^{a}108. I like to take life easy
0 1 2	^{a}109. I try to help other people when I can
0 1 2	110. I wish I were of the opposite sex
0 1 2	111. I keep from getting involved with others
0 1 2	112. I worry a lot

Please write down anything else that describes your feelings, behavior, or interests

Figure 1-2 (cont.) Problem and socially desirable Items 64-112 of the YSR. Superscript *a* indicates socially desirable items.

the same way as responses to the open-ended items on page 2, but they are not scored on the profile.

On several problem items, the youth is asked to describe the problem in question. This enables the user to identify responses that are not properly covered by the item for which they are entered or for which another item is more specific. Examples include 9. *I can't get my mind off certain thoughts*; 46. *Parts of my body twitch or make nervous movements*; and 66. *I repeat certain actions over and over.* On other items, descriptions are requested to enable the user to determine the specific content of the problem the youth is reporting. Examples include 29. *I am afraid of certain animals, situations, or places, other than school*; 40. *I hear sounds or voices that other people think aren't there; 56d. Problems with eyes; 58. I pick my skin or other parts of my body*; 70. *I see things that other people think aren't there*; and 105. *I use alcohol or drugs for nonmedical purposes.* If a youth's description of a problem indicates that the item is scored inappropriately or that the youth scored more than one item for the same problem, only the item that corresponds most precisely to the problem should be counted. (Appendix A provides details of scoring.)

The instructions on page 3 of the YSR state that the ratings should be based on a 6-month period, which is the same as specified for parents' ratings on the CBCL. If a user wishes to obtain reassessments over intervals of less than 6 months, the instructions can be changed to specify shorter periods. For example, if a user wishes to obtain self-ratings before therapy and 3 months later, it is advisable to instruct the youth to base ratings on the previous 3 months each time, so that intervals of the same length are compared.

ADMINISTRATION OF THE YSR

The YSR is designed to be completed by 11- to 18-year-olds having a mental age of at least 10 years and fifth grade reading skills. It is self-explanatory, but someone familiar with the YSR should tell the respondent why it is to be filled out and should be available to answer questions. In most situations, the youth can be told that "I (or we) would like you to fill out this form in order to obtain your views of your interests, feelings, and behavior." The respondent should be assured of confidentiality, which should be strictly guarded. Completed forms should not be accessible to unauthorized people. The structured items usually take about 15 minutes to complete, but respondents who write much on the open-ended items may take longer.

If a youth has poor reading skills, the YSR can be administered orally. If there is a question about the youth's reading skills, the interviewer can hand the YSR to the youth while retaining another copy. The interviewer then says, "I'm going to read these questions to you and I'll write down your answers." After the first few questions, respondents who can read well enough will usually start answering the questions without waiting for them to be asked. Questions about items should be answered in a factual manner aimed at helping the youth understand the specific meaning of items, rather than clinically probing the youth's thoughts. If the YSR is administered orally, it should be done in a private location, out of earshot of others.

SUMMARY

The present revision of the *Manual for the Youth Self-Report* is necessitated by changes in the 1991 profile for scoring the YSR and new provisions for coordinating YSR data with CBCL and TRF data. Pre-1991 editions of the YSR can be scored on the 1991 edition of the YSR profile. Conversely, the 1991 edition of the YSR can be scored on pre-1991 editions of the profile.

The YSR is intended to serve as one component of *multi-axial empirically-based assessment.* Other components include parent- and teacher-reports, standardized tests, physical assessment, observations, and interviews.

The YSR requests 11- to 18-year-olds' reports of their competencies on 17 items similar to those of the CBCL and their problems on 103 items similar to those of the CBCL. It provides a basis for comparing adolescents' views of their own functioning with data from other assessment procedures, such as the CBCL and TRF. Discrepancies between reports by different informants can reveal variations in the youth's functioning in the presence of different informants and in their judgments of the youth's competencies and problems. The YSR is designed to be filled out by adolescents who have a mental age of at least 10 years and fifth grade reading skills, but it can also be administered orally. It can be readministered periodically to assess changes in self-reported functioning.

Chapter 2
Competence Scales

As described in Chapter 1, pages 1 and 2 of the YSR provide items for obtaining self-reports of competencies. These items were shown in Figure 1-1. The items are designed to be scored on Activities, Social, and total competence scales modeled after those for scoring the CBCL/4-18. However, because youths are not asked to report whether they are in a special class or have repeated a grade, there is not a counterpart of the CBCL School scale. Instead, the youth's self-ratings for performance in academic subjects are averaged to form a single item that can be added to the Activities and Social scale scores to yield a total competence score. At least three academic subjects must be rated to qualify for inclusion in the total competence score.

The analyses presented in Chapter 7 revealed that referred youths reported liking to participate in more sports and nonsports activities (Items I and II of the YSR) than did nonreferred youths. This was also true in our analyses for the pre-1991 YSR profile (Achenbach & Edelbrock, 1987). However, the differences on both items were significant in the pre-1991 analyses, whereas only the difference in nonsports activities was significant in the 1991 analyses. Although these two items were counted in the pre-1991 YSR Activities scale, they are omitted from the 1991 version. With the omission of these items, the Activities scale yielded significantly higher scores for nonreferred than for demographically matched referred youths, as reported in Chapter 7. Even though the numbers of sports and nonsports activities are not scored, the self-reports of specific activities can be clinically useful. Furthermore, as the mean scores for participation and skill in sports and nonsports activities were higher for nonreferred than referred youths, they are retained for the Activities scale.

The nature of the competence items makes them less appropriate than our problem items for deriving scales through principal components analyses, as described for the problem items in Chapter 3. This is because scores on some competence items depend partly on other items. On items pertaining to sports, nonsports activities, organizations, and jobs and chores, for example, youths rate the amount and quality of their participation only if they also report that they participate in the specified type of activity.

The scoring rules are designed to minimize artifactual correlations between the *number* of activities of a particular type and *ratings* of quality and amount of participation. For example, a youth who reports liking one sport gets the same score (0) as a youth who reports liking no sports. However, only the youth who likes at least one sport can get a score above 0 for amount and quality of participation. Thus, a score of 0 for number of sports can be accompanied either by a score of 0 or a score above 0 for amount and quality of participation. Furthermore, because scores for amount and quality of participation are averaged over all sports reported, these scores do not automatically increase as the number of sports increases. Nevertheless, it would hardly make sense to use multivariate analyses to find out which of these intrinsically interdependent scores covary to form syndromes as was done with the problem items. Instead, we grouped items into two scales designated as *Activities* and *Social* on the basis of their content.

Appendix A provides hand-scoring instructions for the competence scales of the 1991 YSR profile. If an item is missing from the Social scale, the mean of the other five items of this scale can be substituted for the missing item. However, if any items are missing from the Activities scale, an Activities scale score should not be computed. The total competence score is the sum of the raw scores for the Activities and Social scales, plus the mean for academic performance if the youth has provided ratings for at least three academic subjects. A total competence score should be computed only if scores for the Activities scale, Social scale, and academic performance are available. The competence scales are thus scored like those of the pre-1991 YSR profile, except for the omission of the number of sports and nonsports activities, for which the scores are displayed separately on the profile form.

NORMING THE COMPETENCE SCALES

Normative data for the YSR competence scales were drawn from a subset of subjects in a national sample chosen to be representative of the 48 contiguous states with respect to SES, ethnicity, region, and urban-suburban-rural residence (McConaughy, Stanger, & Achenbach, 1991 provide details). Their parents had participated in a home interview survey regarding their children in 1986. In a home interview survey in the spring of 1989, the parents were administered the CBCL and those subjects who were old enough were asked to complete the YSR. If the subject consented, the interviewer handed the subject the YSR. The interviewer then read the YSR competence items and the first four problem items aloud, writing down the youth's answers on a second copy of the YSR. If it was clear that the youth could read well enough, he or she independently completed the remaining items on pages 3 and 4 of the YSR. If reading skills were questionable, the interviewer continued to read the items aloud and write down the responses.

Of the 1,942 target subjects, 1,719 (88.5%) completed the YSR. A normative sample was constructed by drawing subjects who were 11 to 18 years old when they completed the YSR and who had not received mental health services or special remedial school classes within the preceding 12 months, as reported by their parents. This was done to provide a normative sample of youths who were considered "healthy" in the sense that they had not recently received professional help for behavioral/emotional problems. This criterion may, of course, fail to exclude youths who have significant problems that have not received professional attention for various reasons, including a lack of parental concern. On the other hand, the exclusion criterion of referral for help may inadvertently exclude youths who do not have significant problems but whose parents might be overconcerned. Both these types of errors would reduce the differences that we found between the YSR scores obtained by "healthy" versus "disturbed" youths.

Despite the inevitable error variance in our definitions of both "healthy" and "disturbed" youths, most YSR scale and item scores discriminated very well between referred and nonreferred youths, as documented in Chapters 6 and 7. If a more accurate criterion of truly "healthy" versus truly "disturbed" could be applied in large representative samples like ours, still better discrimination might be found. However, as detailed elsewhere (Achenbach & Edelbrock, 1981), other criteria for distinguishing between normal and deviant samples have not functioned better than referral status.

In our previous work, we used referral for mental health services as the criterion for distinguishing between referred and nonreferred youths. In our current work, we added special education classes for behavioral/emotional problems to the criterion, because Public Law 94-142 (Education of the Handicapped Act, 1977, 1981) now mandates that schools provide special services for students having significant behavioral/emotional problems. As schools have assumed greater responsibility for providing such services, the schools have become key sites for evaluating and intervening with many problems that would previously have been candidates for mental health services outside of school.

Table 2-1 summarizes the demographic characteristics of the 11- to 18-year-olds who comprised the YSR normative samples, after excluding those who had received mental health or special education classes during the previous 12 months.

Table 2-1
Demographic Distribution of YSR
Normative Sample

	Boys 11-18	*Girls 11-18*	*Combined*[b]
	N = 637	678	1,315
SES[a]			
Upper	33%	35%	34%
Middle	45	45	45
Lower	21	21	21
Mean Score	5.4	5.5	5.4
SD of Score	2.2	2.2	2.2
Ethnicity			
White	72%	73%	72%
Black	16	16	16
Hispanic	8	7	8
Other	4	4	4
Region			
Northeast	22%	21%	22%
North Central	27	27	27
South	34	34	34
West	17	18	18

[a]Hollingshead (1975) 9-step scale for parental occupation, using the higher status occupation if both parents were wage earners; scores 1 - 3.5 = lower; 4 - 6.5 = middle; 7 - 9 = upper. If occupational level was unclear, the mean of the two most likely scores was used, resulting in some half-step scores, such as 3.5.
[b]Scores for the combined samples are unweighted means of both sexes.

ASSIGNMENT OF PERCENTILES AND *T* SCORES TO COMPETENCE SCALES

Activities and Social Scale Scores

Figure 2-1 illustrates the competence portion of the 1991 YSR profile scored for 15-year-old David. As can be seen in Figure 2-1, percentiles are displayed on the left side of the competence profile and *T* scores are displayed on the right side.

The percentiles enable the user to compare a youth's raw score on each competence scale shown in the columns of the graphic display with percentiles for the normative samples of the youth's sex. The T scores, which are automatically calculated by the computer-scoring program, provide a metric that is similar for both scales. The intervals on the left side of the profile encompass differing numbers of percentiles in order to correctly correspond to the T score intervals on the right side of the profile. (The next section can be skipped by readers uninterested in how T scores were assigned. Chapter 10 discusses the use of raw scores versus T scores for statistical purposes.)

The percentiles indicated on the 1991 profile were derived according to a procedure designed to produce smoother, more normal distributions of percentile scores than were generated for the pre-1991 versions of the profile. According to this procedure, a raw score that falls at a particular percentage of the cumulative frequency distribution is assumed to span all the next lower percentiles down to the percentile occupied by the next lower raw score in the distribution (Crocker & Algina, 1986). To represent this span of percentiles, each raw score is assigned to the midpoint of the percentiles that it spans. As shown in Figure 2-1, for example, David obtained a score of 4.5 on the Activities scale. A score of 4.5 or lower was obtained by 41.9% of 11- to 18-year-old boys in our normative sample. The next higher raw score, 5.0, was obtained by 15.4% of the boys in our normative sample. The *cumulative percent* of boys obtaining a raw score of 4.5 or lower was thus 41.9%, while the cumulative percent obtaining a raw score of 5.0 or lower was 41.9% + 15.4% = 57.3%. The interval from raw score 4.5 to raw score 5.0 thus spanned from a cumulative percent of 41.9% to 57.3%. To represent this interval in terms of a percentile at the midpoint of the interval, we took the cumulative percent at the top of the interval (57.3%) and subtracted the cumulative percent at the bottom of the interval (41.9%), i.e., 57.3% minus 41.9% = 15.4. To obtain the

1991 YSR Profile for Boys & Girls — Competence Scales

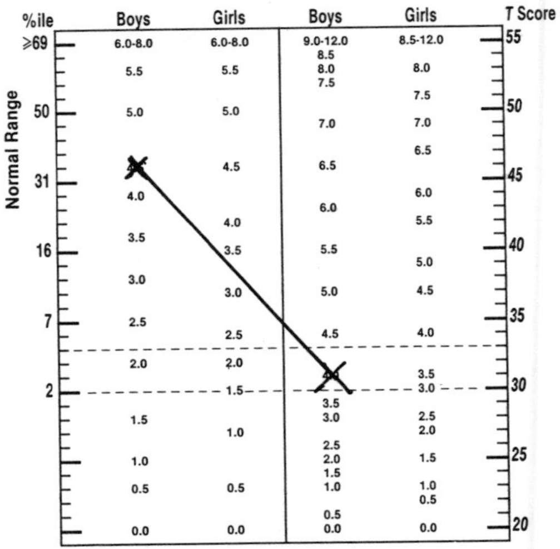

Name David

ID # 83591

Age 15

Date YSR Filled Out 4-4-91

Total Competence Score

Activities 4.5

Social 4.0

Academic + 1.5

Total 10.0

Total *T* from Table 33

Broken lines = borderline clinical range

Not scored on competence scales
1 I A. Number of sports
2 IIA. Number of nonsports activities

ACTIVITIES

2 I. B. Mean sports partic. & skill
0.5 II. B. Mean non-sports partic. & skill
1 IV.A. # of jobs
1 B Mean job quality
4.5 Total

SOCIAL

0 III.A. # of organiz.
0 B. Mean partic. in organiz.
1 V. 1. # of friends
1 2. Contacts w. friends
1 VI.A. Behav. w. others
1 B. Alone
4 Total

Total Competence Scores

Boys	*T*	Girls	*T*
23.0	80	23.0	80
22.5	79	22.5	79
22.0	78	22.0	78
21.5	77	21.5	77
21.0	76	21.0	74
20.5	74	20.5	71
20.0	71	20.0	69
19.5	69	19.5	67
19.0	67	19.0	65
18.5	65	18.5	64
18.0	63	18.0	62
17.5	62	17.5	60
17.0	60	17.0	58
16.5	58	16.5	56
16.0	56	16.0	54
15.5	54	15.5	53
15.0	52	15.0	51
14.5	50	14.5	49
14.0	48	14.0	48
13.5	47	13.5	46
13.0	45	13.0	45
12.5	43	12.5	43
12.0	41	12.0	41
11.5	40	11.5	40
11.0	38	11.0	38
10.5	36	10.5	37
10.0	33	10.0	35
9.5	32	9.5	33
9.0	30	9.0	32
8.5	29	8.5	30
8.0	28	8.0	29
7.5	27	7.5	28
7.0	26	7.0	26
6.5	24	6.5	25
6.0	23	6.0	24
5.5	22	5.5	23
5.0	21	5.0	22
4.5	20	4.5	21
4.0	19	4.0	19
3.5	18	3.5	18
3.0	17	3.0	17
2.5	16	2.5	16
2.0	14	2.0	15
1.5	13	1.5	14
1.0	12	1.0	12
0.5	11	0.5	11
0.0	10	0.0	10

Figure 2-1. Hand-scored YSR competence profile for 15-year-old David.

midpoint, we then divided this difference in half and added it to the lower percent, i.e., 41.9% + 7.7% = 49.6. This corresponds to the following formula provided by Crocker and Algina (1986, p. 439):

$$P = \frac{cf_l + .5(f_i)}{N} \; X \; 100\%$$

where P = percentile; cf_l is the cumulative frequency for all scores lower than the score of interest; f_i is the frequency of scores in the interval of interest; and N is the number in the sample.

After obtaining the midpoint percentile in this way, we used the procedure provided by Abramowitz and Stegun (1968) to assign a normalized T score of 50 to the 49.6th percentile for the raw score of 5.0. In Figure 2-1, the raw score of 5.0 is therefore on the same line as the T score of 50 on the right side of the profile.

The main effect of using the midpoint percentile rather than the cumulative percentile on the syndrome scales was to provide a smoother, less skewed, and more differentiated basis for T scores.

The raw scores of the YSR competence scales were *negatively skewed* in the normative samples. That is, a large proportion of nonreferred children received relatively high competence scores. Furthermore, *low* scores are clinically significant on the competence scales. To take account of the negatively skewed distributions and the need for finer differentiation between low scores than between high scores on the competence scales, we assigned T scores to the competence scales in the following ways:

1. At the top end of each competence scale, we assigned a T score of 55 to all raw scores at the 69th percentile and above. We did this to prevent overinterpretation of

differences between scores that are at the high end of the normal range.

2. At the low end of the scales, we based T scores on percentiles down to the second percentile (T score = 30). We then divided the remaining raw scores into T score intervals down to a T score of 20. Because there are not many raw scores below the second percentile of the competence scales, we assigned the low competence scores a range of only 10 T scores (29 through 20). Broken lines at T scores of 30 and 33 demarcate a borderline clinical range that spans from about the second to the fifth percentile of the normative sample. This range was chosen to approximate the same degree of deviance from the middle of the normative sample as is represented by the borderline clinical range from $T = 67$ to $T = 70$ for the syndrome scales described in Chapter 3. The borderline ranges were chosen to provide efficient discrimination between demographically matched referred and nonreferred samples (described in Chapter 6), while minimizing the number of "false positives," i.e., normal children who score in the clinical range. If maximum discrimination is sought between deviant and nondeviant children without regard to the increase in false positives, cutpoints above $T = 33$ on the competence scales may improve discrimination in some samples.

Looking again at David's profile in Figure 2-1, you can see that David obtained a raw score of 4.0 on the Social scale. As can be seen from the left side of the profile, a raw score of 4.0 on the Social scale falls just above the 2nd percentile for boys. As shown on the right side of the profile, this is equivalent to a T score of 31. Because T scores from 30 to 33 are in the borderline clinical range demarcated by the broken lines on the profile, David's score is low enough to be of concern, although it is not below $T = 30$, where deviance is indicated with more certainty.

As shown in Figure 2-1, the mean of David's ratings for academic subjects was 1.5. T scores are not assigned to academic performance, but the raw score for academic performance is included in the total competence score, as explained in the following section.

Total Competence Score

The YSR total competence score is the sum of the raw scores for the Activities and Social scales, plus the mean score for ratings of performance in academic subjects. If any of these three scores is missing, a total competence score is not computed.

Percentiles and T scores were assigned to the total YSR competence scores in the same way as done for the scores on the competence scales, except that the top end of the total competence scale was not truncated at a T score of 55. Midpoint percentiles for the raw total competence scores were computed in the manner described previously for problem scores. Normalized T scores were then assigned from the 2nd percentile ($T = 30$) to the highest possible raw score, which was assigned a T score of 80. Raw scores below the 2nd percentile were divided into equal intervals for assignment to T scores from 10 through 29. On the hand-scored profile, a table to the right of the graphic display lists the T score for each possible raw score. The computer-scoring program automatically computes the T score for the total competence score. T scores <37 are considered to be clearly in the clinical range, whereas T scores from 37 to 40 are in the borderline clinical range. The borderline range is indicated by broken lines in the box to the right of the hand-scored profile. The computer-scored profile displays a + with total competence scores that are in the borderline range and ++ with scores that are in the clinical range.

Table 2-2 presents the mean, standard deviation, and standard error of the mean for the raw scores and T scores obtained by our normative samples on each competence scale.

Table 2-2

Competence Scale Scores for YSR Normative Sample

| | 637 Boys | | | | | | 678 Girls | | | | | |
| | Raw Score | | | T Score | | | Raw Score | | | T Score | | |
Scale	Mean	SD	SE[a]	Mean	SD	SE[a]	Mean	SD	SE[a]	Mean	SD	SE[a]
Activities	4.8	1.4	.1	47.9	7.2	.3	4.9	1.3	.1	48.1	7.2	.3
Social	7.3	1.8	.1	47.9	7.1	.3	7.3	2.0	.1	48.0	7.3	.3
Total Comp	14.4	2.7	.1	50.2	9.9	.4	14.6	2.9	.1	50.1	9.9	.4

Note. Ns vary because of missing data for some scales; e.g., youths not attending school were not included in Total Competence score.

[a]SE = standard error of the mean.

SUMMARY

Scales entitled *Activities* and *Social* are provided for scoring the competence items on pages 1 and 2 of the YSR. The YSR total competence score comprises the sum of the two scale scores, plus the mean of the youth's self-ratings for academic performance. Because the numbers of sports and nonsports activities were not significantly lower for referred than non-referred youths, these items are not included in the 1991 YSR competence scales.

The normative samples for the 1991 profile scales were described and their mean raw and T scores for each scale were presented. The procedures for assigning percentiles and T scores to the 1991 scale scores were detailed and illustrated on the competence portion of the 1991 YSR profile.

Chapter 3
Syndrome and Total Problem Scales

Beside enabling youths to describe themselves in terms of many specific items, the YSR is designed to identify syndromes of problems that tend to occur together. A primary reason for developing the family of instruments that includes the YSR was to provide an empirical foundation for identifying syndromes from which to construct a taxonomy of disorders. The word *syndrome* refers to problems that tend to occur together, without any assumptions about the nature or causes of disorders. Rather than imposing *a priori* assumptions about what syndromes exist, we derived syndromes quantitatively from problem items scored for clinically referred youths on the YSR, as well as on the CBCL and TRF. Findings for the pre-1991 edition of the YSR profile have been reported by Achenbach and Edelbrock (1987), while findings for the 1991 CBCL and TRF have been reported in the Manuals for those instruments (Achenbach, 1991b, 1991c).

To derive the syndromes, we applied principal components analyses to the correlations among items. Like factor analysis, principal components analysis is used to identify groups of items whose scores covary with one another. However, in factor analysis, the obtained correlations among items are reduced to reflect only the variance each item has in common with all other items. The estimate of the item's "communality" (the variance it has in common with other items) typically consists of the square of the item's multiple correlation with all other items. In principal components analysis, by contrast, the obtained correlation of each item with each other item is taken at face value rather than being reduced according to an estimate of communality.

Because we wanted to focus on the associations that were actually obtained among items in large samples, we did not want the associations among particular items to be differentially reduced by the degree to which the items happened to correlate with all other items. When the number of items is as large as we used, the results of principal components analyses are generally similar to the results of principal factor analyses anyway (Gorsuch, 1983).

PRE-1991 SYNDROMES

To reflect possible sex differences in the prevalence and patterning of problems, we performed separate principal components analyses of the problem items reported by clinically referred youths of each sex at ages 11 to 18. Because all 102 specific problem items were reported to be present by at least 5% of the clinical sample of each sex, all the items were included in the components analyses, except the open-ended item 56h. *Other physical problems.*

We applied orthogonal (varimax) rotations to the principal components matrices ranging from 6 to 15 components in order to identify sets of problems that remained relatively intact despite changes in the number of components. We then chose the rotation that included the most representative sets of problem items found for boys and girls, respectively. These items formed the basis for the syndrome scales for that sex.

Note that the pre-1991 syndrome scales for each sex were based directly on the rotated components for that sex, whether or not the syndromes were the same for both sexes. In fact, six syndromes were found that were similar enough to be given the same names for both sexes, although the items comprising the syndromes differed somewhat between the sexes. A seventh syndrome, designated as *Self-Destructive/Identity Problems* was found for boys but did not have a clear counterpart among girls.

DERIVATION OF THE 1991 SYNDROMES

In deriving the pre-1991 syndromes for the YSR, CBCL, and TRF, we sought to capture possible differences in the patterning of problems that might occur among different sex/age groups, as seen by different informants. As the development and applications of our instruments have advanced, it has become more important to coordinate assessment of children and youth of both sexes as seen from different perspectives. Syndrome scales that are more uniform for both sexes, different ages, and multiple instruments would make it easier for practitioners to keep track of the syndromes being assessed. The common elements of syndromes derived from the different instruments would also provide the basis for taxonomic constructs that transcend specific instruments. Such constructs would serve as foci for research and theory from diverse perspectives.

As part of our effort to integrate assessment across both sexes, different age groups, and different informants, we performed new principal components analyses of YSRs obtained from clinical samples of 709 boys and 563 girls at ages 11 to 18. These samples included YSRs that had been analyzed for the previous edition of the YSR profile (Achenbach & Edelbrock, 1987), plus additional YSRs obtained from youths referred for mental health services since then.

The subjects were seen in 26 settings, including guidance clinics, university child psychiatric clinics, community mental health centers, private practices, and inpatient services. The settings were mostly in the eastern United States but included some as far west as Utah. They provided a broad distribution of socioeconomic, demographic, and other client characteristics that should minimize selective factors affecting the caseloads of individual services. On Hollingshead's (1975) 9-step scale for parental occupation, the mean SES was 5.0, (SD = 2.5), averaged across the distributions for boys and girls. Ethnic distribution averaged across the two sexes was 78% white, 17% black, and 5% other. (The following sections can be skipped by readers uninterested in how the 1991 syndromes were derived.)

Principal Components Analyses

Two principal components analyses were performed on the sample of each sex. The first analysis resembled the analyses used to develop the previous edition of the YSR profile. This analysis employed all 102 specific problem items. The second principal components analysis for each sex was designed to identify syndromes that had counterparts in ratings by parents and teachers, as well as self-ratings by youths. These analyses therefore employed only the 89 problem items that have counterparts on the CBCL and TRF, as well as being on the YSR.

Rotations of Principal Components

After performing principal components analyses, we subjected the largest 6 to 15 components from each analysis to orthogonal (varimax) rotations. (Rotations of principal components are transformations of their item loadings designed to approximate the ideal of "simple structure" — that is, to divide the items that were analyzed into a few tightly knit groups of strongly interrelated items.) Although the varimax criterion for simple structure avoids correlations among rotated components, this does not preclude correlations among the sets of high loading items that are retained from the rotated components to form syndrome scales. In fact, as discussed later, the final syndrome scales do correlate positively with each other.

For each sex, the 6- to 15-component rotations were examined to identify sets of items that consistently grouped together with high loadings on a rotated component. Four to five rotations were selected that included representative versions of these components. The items loading ≥.30 on these components were then listed side-by-side to identify the version of each component that included the maximum number of high loading items which also loaded highly on the other versions. (On the CBCL and TRF, a syndrome designated as Aggressive Behavior had so many high loading items that only items loading ≥.40 were retained; although a similar syndrome was found in the YSR analyses, items loading ≥.30 were retained because the YSR Aggressive syndrome did not account for such a large proportion of variance as did the CBCL and TRF versions.)

After selecting the two to three best versions of each rotated component, we identified the rotation that included the largest proportion of the best versions of each component. The versions of the rotated components found in this rotation were used to represent the syndromes for the sex for which the analysis was done.

As an example, we performed a principal components analysis of the 102 YSR problem items scored by 709 clinically referred boys. We then identified syndromes of items that tended to occur together, as reflected in their high loadings on a particular component. We selected the 10-, 11-, 12-, and 13-component rotations as including the best examples of these syndromes of high loading items.

One syndrome was designated as *Somatic Complaints*, because most of the items loading ≥.30 involved somatic problems. From the versions of this syndrome found in the 10-, 11-, 12-, and 13-component rotations, we listed items that loaded ≥.30 on any of the four versions. We found that two of the four versions had exactly the same 13 items loading ≥.30. On one other version, one of the 13 items fell below .30 and was replaced by another item. The remaining version had three additional items loading ≥.30. Based on the similarities among their Somatic Complaints syndromes, these three rotations all became equal candidates for retention. The same procedure was followed for each of the other syndromes that appeared in multiple rotations of the components obtained from the boys' YSRs.

When we tabulated the number of syndromes whose best versions occurred in each rotation, we found that the 12-component rotation had the largest proportion of the "best" versions of the syndromes. We therefore retained the versions of the syndromes that were identified in the 12-component rotation. As explained in the following sections, these were then compared with syndromes from other analyses to identify items to be retained for the syndrome scales.

Recall now that a second principal components analysis was performed on the YSR sample for each sex. To identify "cross-informant" syndromes that were common to the YSR, CBCL, and TRF, the second principal components analyses employed only the 89 problem items that are common to the three instruments. Varimax rotations were performed on the largest 6 to 15 components obtained for each sex. The procedures outlined earlier were then used to identify the syndromes that would serve as the YSR candidates for the cross-informant syndromes. We thus obtained two sets of syndromes for each sex. For the boys, for example, one set was derived from the analyses of 102 items, while the second set was derived from the analysis of the 89 common items.

Derivation of Core Syndromes

The syndromes derived from the two sets of analyses for each sex represent two alternative ways of viewing the patterns of problems. The analyses of all the items specific to the YSR might detect patterns that may not be detectible in the subset of items common to the YSR, CBCL, and TRF. The analyses of the common items, on the other hand, might identify patterns that are also detectible in CBCL and TRF ratings.

To determine whether syndromes were evident only in the analyses of the full set of YSR items, we compared the syndromes obtained from these analyses with the syndromes

obtained from the analyses of the subset of common items. All
the YSR syndromes had counterparts in both the 102- and 89-
item sets. However, a syndrome designated as *Self-Destruc-
tive/Identity Problems* was found only for boys on the YSR and
was not found in the CBCL or TRF analyses. This syndrome
had also been found for boys in the analyses for the pre-1991
YSR profile (Achenbach & Edelbrock, 1987). Seven other
syndromes were found in the analyses of both the full set of
items and the common-item subset. Table 3-1 lists the names
of the syndromes and the mean of their eigenvalues obtained in
the varimax rotation of the full set of items.

Table 3-1
Syndromes Retained from Principal
Components/Varimax Analyses of the YSR[a]

Internalizing	*Neither Int nor Ext*	*Externalizing*
Somatic Complaints (4.70)	Social Problems (3.50)	Delinquent Behavior (3.44)
Anxious/ Depressed (8.35)	Thought Problems (3.32)	Aggressive Behavior (5.54)
	Attention Problems (2.50)	
	Self-Destruct/Identity Problems[b](2.65)	

Note. Internalizing and Externalizing groupings were derived from second-order
analyses, as explained in Chapter 4. The mean of the eigenvalues for both sexes
is shown in parentheses.
[a]A syndrome designated as Withdrawn is also scored on the Internalizing section
of the 1991 YSR profile because it met the criteria for a cross-informant
syndrome based on the CBCL and TRF findings.
[b]The Self-Destructive/Identity Problems syndrome was found only for boys.

There were some differences between the items comprising
the versions of syndromes obtained from the analyses of the
full set and those obtained from the common-item subset.
There were also differences among the versions of each
syndrome found for boys and girls. To identify *core syndromes* that underlay these variations, we made side-by-side

lists of the items of syndromes that had been obtained from each sex in both the full set and the common-item analyses. We then determined which items were found in the corresponding syndrome for both sexes. The Somatic Complaints syndrome, for example, was found for both sexes. We therefore constructed the core Somatic Complaints syndrome from items that were found in versions of this syndrome for both sexes. An item was counted as present for boys or for girls if it was found in either the full set or common-item version of the syndrome for that group.

The core syndromes were used in the following ways:

1. They provided the items for the 1991 syndrome scales. Thus, scales were constructed for the seven syndromes that were found for both sexes, plus the one syndrome that was found only for boys. The items comprising the core syndromes are used to score the seven syndromes for both sexes.

2. The core versions of the YSR syndromes found in the common-item subset were compared with common-item core syndromes from the CBCL and TRF to identify syndromes that were similar in two or more instruments.

Cross-Informant Syndromes

A major aim of the 1991 profiles is to provide common foci for assessing children from the perspectives of self-, parent-, and teacher-reports. These common foci consist of syndromes that were identified as having counterparts in the principal components analyses of the YSR, CBCL, and TRF, or any two of these three instruments. Core syndromes were constructed from the syndromes derived from the CBCL and TRF by the method just described for the YSR (details are provided by Achenbach, 1991b, 1991c).

To identify items that were common to the core syndromes of two or more informants, we made side-by-side lists of the items comprising the corresponding core syndromes from the different instruments. Items that were found on core syndromes for at least two of the three instruments were used to form a *cross-informant syndrome construct*. For example, items of the core Somatic Complaints syndromes derived from the YSR, CBCL, and TRF were listed side-by-side. Nine items were found to be common to the core Somatic Complaints syndrome from at least two of the three instruments. These nine items were used to define a cross-informant syndrome construct which could be assessed via the Somatic Complaints scales of the YSR, CBCL, and TRF.

The term "construct" is used to indicate that the common items represent a hypothetical variable. In statistical language, the term "latent variable" is used for variables of this sort. Because none of the core Somatic Complaints syndromes for the individual instruments included any additional items, the Somatic Complaints scales for the YSR, CBCL, and TRF have the same nine items. However, the Somatic Complaints scales are normed separately for the YSR, CBCL, and TRF, as described later.

For some cross-informant constructs, the core syndrome of a particular instrument did include items beside those that qualified for the cross-informant construct. Because these items were associated with the syndrome in ratings by a particular type of informant, they were retained for the syndrome scale to be scored by that type of informant. As an example, for the cross-informant construct designated as *Thought Problems*, the CBCL core syndrome included item *80. Stares blankly*. This item is not on the YSR, because it did not seem sensible to ask youths to report whether they stare blankly. It is on the TRF, but did not qualify for the TRF core syndrome. Because it was associated with the CBCL Thought Problems syndrome in a majority of the sex/age groups, it is scored on the CBCL Thought Problems scale even though it is not part of the cross-informant construct and is not scored on the YSR or TRF Thought Problems scales. Other items were also retained on particular scales for one instrument to capture aspects of a syndrome that might be evident to only one type of informant.

A syndrome designated as *Withdrawn* was found in the CBCL and TRF analyses, but not in the YSR analyses. Because it met our cross-informant criteria by being found for two out of the three types of informants, it is included on the profiles for scoring the YSR, as well as the profiles for the CBCL and TRF. However, because we did not find a counterpart of the Withdrawn syndrome in self-ratings, some users may prefer to ignore the YSR scores obtained for this syndrome. Table 3-2 summarizes the steps in constructing the 1991 syndrome scales.

PROFILES FOR SCORING
THE 1991 SYNDROMES

The 1991 profiles for the YSR, CBCL, and TRF display the items of the eight cross-informant syndromes that are scored from ratings by youths, parents, and teachers, respectively. To facilitate comparisons among reports by the different informants, the syndromes are arranged in the same order on all three profiles. A computer program is available that scores and compares data from any combination of father-, mother-, youth-, and teacher-reports (details are provided by Achenbach, 1991a). The syndromes that were found in ratings by only one type of informant are not displayed on the profiles, because they comprise relatively rare problems and their distributions of scores do not lend themselves to a profile approach. However, the computer-scoring programs compute total scores and T scores for these scales, and the hand-scoring profiles provide spaces to enter the scores for them.

Table 3-2
Steps in Deriving 1991 YSR Syndrome Scales

1. Two sets of principal components analyses were performed on YSR problem items for clinically referred youths of each sex.

   a. Set 1—principal components analysis of all YSR problem items.

   b. Set 2—principal components analysis of 89 problem items common to CBCL, YSR, TRF.

2. Varimax rotations of 6 to 15 components from each analysis.

3. Identification of groups of items that remained together throughout multiple rotations.

4. Selection of rotation that included the largest proportion of the best versions of groups of co-occurring items.

5. Derivation of *core syndromes* from items found in the versions of a syndrome for both sexes.

6. Derivation of *cross-informant syndrome constructs* from items common to core syndromes for at least two of the three instruments (CBCL, YSR, TRF).

7. Construction of YSR syndrome scales consisting of YSR items for the eight cross-informant constructs, plus *Self-Destructive/Identity Problems* scale scored only from YSR for boys.

8. Assignment of normalized *T* scores based on percentiles of normative samples, separately for each sex.

Figure 3-1 shows the problem scales of a computer-scored profile for 15-year-old David. (Appendix A provides hand-scoring instructions.) The eight syndromes displayed on the profile have counterparts that bear the same names on the 1991 profiles for the CBCL and TRF. Chapter 4 presents the basis for designating scales I-III as Internalizing and scales VII-VIII as Externalizing.

The items comprising each scale are listed under the title of the scale. A total scale score is computed by summing the 1s and 2s scored by the youth for the scale's items. Asterisks indicate items on the YSR version of a cross-informant syndrome scale that are not on the CBCL or TRF versions. On syndrome scale *II. Anxious/Depressed*, for example, the asterisk beside item *18*, which is abbreviated as *Harmself* on the profile, indicates that it was included in the core syndrome derived from the analyses of both sexes scored on the YSR, but not in the core syndromes scored from the CBCL or TRF. Item 18 is therefore scored on the YSR Anxious/Depressed scale but not on the CBCL or TRF Anxious/Depressed scales. On the right side of the profile, *T* scores are shown that indicate how a particular scale score compares with scores obtained by normative samples of youths. Later sections of this chapter explain how the *T* scores were assigned. Items that are not scored on syndrome scales I-VIII are listed to the right of the profile under the heading *Other Problems*.

Beside the eight scales for scoring syndromes that have counterparts on the CBCL and TRF, the YSR scoring program computes raw scores and *T* scores for Scale *IX. Self-Destructive/Identity Problems* for boys. On the computer printout, a $ is printed to the right of each item that is counted in this scale. This scale is viewed as optional, because it was found only in self-ratings by boys. Furthermore, the items of this scale have low prevalence rates, and most boys have low scores on the scale. As a consequence, the Self-Destructive/Identity Problems scale does not lend itself to the specification of normal, borderline, and clinical ranges like those specified for Scales I-

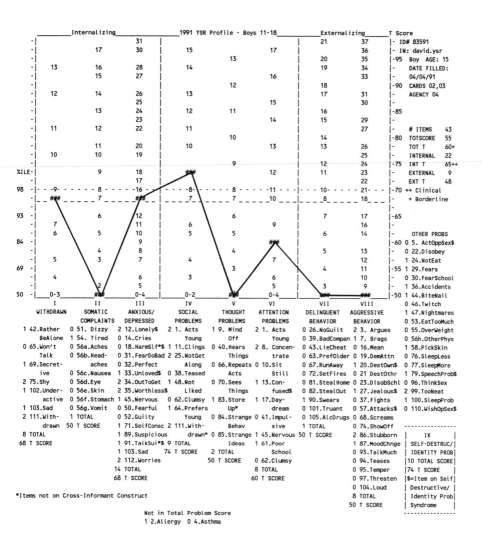

Figure 3-1. Computer-scored YSR problem profile for 15-year-old David.

VIII. Although *T* scores can be computed for the scale, these provide only guidelines as to whether a boy scores himself at relatively low, medium, or high levels, as compared to a normative sample of peers. (Appendix A provides hand-scoring instructions and *T* scores for Scale IX.)

As shown at the bottom of the profile in Figure 3-1, Items *2. Allergy* and *4. Asthma* are not included on the problem scales. This is because they did not discriminate significantly between referred and nonreferred youths in self-ratings (analyses are presented in Chapter 7), or in parent-ratings either (Achenbach, 1991b). However, the scores for these items are displayed, because it may be clinically important to know whether a youth has allergies or asthma.

Scores for Internalizing and Externalizing are computed by summing Scales I-III and VII-VIII, respectively. Because Item *103. Unhappy, sad, or depressed* is scored both on Scale I and Scale III, its score is subtracted from the sum of Scales I, II, and III in order to avoid counting it twice in the Internalizing score. Raw scores and *T* scores for Internalizing and Externalizing, as well as for the total problem score, are displayed in a table to the right of the profile (not shown in Figure 3-1).

ASSIGNING NORMALIZED *T* SCORES TO SYNDROME SCALES

This section can be skipped by readers uninterested how *T* scores were assigned.

Lowest *T* Scores

For each syndrome scale, we computed percentiles using the same procedure and normative samples as were described in Chapter 2 for the competence scales. On some syndrome scales, a large percentage of the normative sample obtained scores of 0 or 1. On other syndrome scales, much smaller percentages of the normative sample obtained very low scores. If we assigned normalized *T* scores solely on the basis of percentiles, some scales would start at much lower scores than other scales would. When displayed on a profile, the different starting points for the scales could lead to misleading impressions. For example, if a youth obtained a raw score of 0 on a scale that started at a *T* score of 28 and a raw score of 0 on a scale that started at a *T* score of 50, it might appear that the youth scored higher on the second scale than on the first. Yet, the youth had no problems on either scale.

To avoid misleading impressions of this sort and to prevent overinterpretation of differences among scores in the low normal range, we truncated the assignment of *T* scores to the syndrome scales. According to the midpoint percentiles, no syndrome scales would have required a *T* score higher than 50, which is equivalent to the 50th percentile. To equalize the starting points of all the syndrome scales, we assigned a *T* score of 50 to all raw scores that fell at midpoint percentiles ≤50. As an example, on Scale *V. Thought Problems* for boys, only a raw score of 0 fell ≤50th percentile. On Scale *VIII. Aggressive Behavior*, by contrast, raw scores of 0-8 were all ≤50th percentile. All these scores were therefore assigned a *T* score of 50, as shown in Figure 3-1.

The assignment of a *T* score of 50 to several raw scores reduces the differentiation among low scores on scales such as the *Aggressive Behavior* scale. Loss of this differentiation is of little clinical importance, because it involves small differences that are all at the low end of the normal range. If differentiation at the low end is nevertheless desired for assessing differences that are within the normal range, raw scale scores may be used in place of *T* scores. For statistical analyses, raw scores are usually preferable, because they directly reflect all differences among individuals without any truncation or other transformations.

Highest *T* Scores

Most youths in the normative samples obtained scores that were well below the maximum possible on each syndrome scale. It was therefore impossible to base *T* scores on percentiles at the high end of the syndrome scales. On the *Aggressive Behavior* scale shown in Figure 3-1, for example, the maximum possible score is 38, but 98% of the normative sample of boys obtained scores ≤21. Furthermore, most of the scores from 22 to 38 were not obtained by any youths in the normative sample. Basing *T* scores on percentiles above the 98th percentile would thus not really reflect differences among scores obtained by youths in the normative sample. We therefore based *T* scores on percentiles only up to a *T* score of 70.

For the highest scores on the syndrome scales, we assigned *T* scores from 71 to 100 in as many increments as there were remaining raw scores on the scale. For example, on the *Aggressive Behavior* scale for boys, the raw score of 21 was assigned a *T* score of 70. Because there are 19 items on the scale, the maximum possible score is 38 (i.e., if a boy received a score of 2 on all 19 items, his raw scale score would be 38). There are 30 intervals from 71 to 100, but only 17 possible raw scores from 22 through 38. To assign *T* scores to the 17 raw scores, we divided 30 by 20. Because 30/20 = 1.76, *T* scores were assigned to raw scores in intervals of 1.76. Thus, a raw score of 22 was assigned a *T* score of 70 + 1.76 = 71.76, rounded off to 72. A raw score of 23 was assigned a *T* score of 71.76 + 1.76 = 73.52 rounded to 74, and so on.

Because of the skewed raw score distributions, truncation of low scores at *T* = 50, and assignment of high *T* scores in equal intervals, the mean *T* scores of the syndrome scales are above 50 and their standard deviations are below 10. They thus do not conform to the mean of 50 and standard deviation of 10 expected when normal distributions are transformed directly into *T* scores. The means and standard deviations also differ between normative and clinical samples, of course.

Table 3-3 presents the means, standard deviations, and standard errors for the normative samples. Appendix B presents the corresponding data for all YSR scale scores obtained by demographically matched normative and clinical samples of each sex.

ASSIGNING NORMALIZED *T* SCORES TO TOTAL PROBLEM SCORES

We based normalized *T* scores on midpoint percentiles of the total problem score in much the same way as described for the syndrome scales, with the following two differences:

1. The total number of problem items is much greater than the number of items on any syndrome scale, and at least some problems are reported for most youths. Consequently, very few youths in our normative samples obtained extremely low total problem scores. It was therefore unnecessary to set a minimum *T* score at which to group low raw scores as we did for the syndrome scales. Instead, we based normalized *T* scores directly on percentiles of the distribution of total problem scores obtained by our normative samples, up to the 97.7th percentile (*T* = 70).

2. No youth in either our normative or clinical samples obtained a total problem score approaching the maximum possible of 202. If we assigned *T* scores above 70 by dividing all the top raw scores into the 30 intervals from 71 to 100, we would have compressed scores actually obtained by our clinical samples into a narrow range of *T* scores. We would also have assigned raw scores above those actually obtained to a broad range of *T* scores. For example, the highest total score obtained in our sample of clinically referred girls

Table 3-3
Problem Scale Scores for YSR Normative Sample

| | 637 Boys | | | | | | 678 Girls | | | | | |
| | Raw Score | | | T Score | | | Raw Score | | | T Score | | |
Scale	Mean	SD	SE[a]	Mean	SD	SE[a]	Mean	SD	SE[a]	Mean	SD	SE[a]
Withdrawn	3.4	2.2	.1	53.8	5.7	.2	4.0	2.4	.1	54.0	5.9	.2
Somatic Comp	2.2	2.3	.1	54.1	6.0	.2	2.9	2.9	.1	53.9	5.8	.2
Anxious/Depressed	5.1	4.2	.2	54.1	6.0	.2	6.4	5.1	.2	54.0	6.2	.2
Social Probs	2.6	2.0	.1	53.8	5.5	.2	2.5	2.1	.1	53.9	5.8	.2
Thought Probs	2.3	2.1	.1	54.0	6.1	.2	2.4	2.3	.1	54.0	5.9	.2
Attention Probs	4.8	3.0	.1	54.0	6.0	.2	4.6	3.0	.1	54.0	5.9	.2
Delinquent Behav	3.2	2.5	.1	54.0	6.0	.2	2.5	2.2	.1	53.9	5.7	.2
Aggressive Behav	8.5	5.2	.2	54.0	5.9	.2	7.9	4.9	.2	54.0	5.9	.2
Self Destructive[b]	1.9	2.1	.1	54.0	5.9	.2	—	—	—	—	—	—
Internalizing	10.5	7.0	.3	50.1	10.0	.4	12.9	8.5	.3	50.1	9.9	.4
Externalizing	11.6	7.0	.3	49.9	9.8	.4	10.3	6.3	.2	50.0	9.8	.4
Total Problems	37.3	19.1	.8	50.1	9.9	.4	38.9	21.3	.8	50.1	10.1	.4

[a]SE = standard error of the mean.
[b]Self-Destructive/Identity Problems scale scored for boys only.

was 151. If we had assigned T scores in equal intervals from 70 to 100, only 17 T scores would have been allocated to the range of 64 raw scores actually found in our clinical sample, whereas 13 T scores would have been allocated to the 51 raw scores above those actually found.

To enable the upper T scores to reflect differences among the raw scores that are most likely to occur, we assigned a T score of 89 for each sex to the mean of the five highest raw scores found in the clinical sample from which the core syndromes were derived. (In contrast to the use of the single highest score in the pre-1991 profiles, we used the mean of the five highest scores to reduce the effect of single extreme outliers.) The raw scores ranging from $T = 70$ to the mean of the five highest scores were then assigned T scores in equal intervals from 71 through 89. The raw scores above the mean of the five highest were assigned T scores in equal intervals from 90 through 100. The T score assigned to each raw total problem score is displayed in a box to the right of the hand-scored profile and is printed out by the computer-scoring program.

NORMAL, BORDERLINE, AND CLINICAL RANGES

Syndrome Scales

As shown in Figure 3-1, broken lines are printed across the profile at the T scores of 67 and 70. These represent a borderline range in which scores are not so clearly in the normal range as those that are below $T = 67$, nor so clearly in the clinical range as those that are above $T = 70$. This borderline range is analogous to the one shown in Figure 2-1 for the competence scales. Just as with the competence scales, there is no well-validated criterion for categorically distinguishing between youths who are "normal" and those who are "abnormal" with respect to each syndrome. Because youths are continually changing and because all assessment procedures are subject to error of measurement and other limitations, no single score precisely indicates a youth's status. Instead, a score on a syndrome scale should be interpreted as an estimate of the youth's status as reported by the youth when the YSR is completed.

The test-retest reliability of YSR self-ratings is satisfactory (Chapter 5) and the standard error of measurement is generally small (Appendix B). This means that, on the average, the range of scores represented by a particular score is relatively narrow. Nevertheless, in deciding whether a youth is clinically deviant on a particular syndrome, it is important to remember that each score is merely one point on a continuum of quantitative variation. It is especially important to be aware of such variation when a score is intermediate between the normal and clinical range. When a syndrome score is between the broken lines, it should therefore be described as "borderline clinical."

If a specific categorical cutpoint is desired for statistical purposes, the T score of 67 can be used to represent the bottom of the clinical range. As shown in Chapter 6, T scores of 67 significantly discriminated between referred and nonreferred youths on the eight cross-informant syndromes scored from the YSR. Furthermore, there were significant differences between the proportions of referred and nonreferred youths scoring in the normal, borderline, and clinical ranges. These findings support the cutpoint of $T = 67$ and the tripartite division into the normal, borderline, and clinical ranges. However, other cutpoints and borderline ranges can be tried for research on the constructs represented by the syndrome scales.

Total Problem Score

To test the discriminative efficiency of various cutpoints, we used a Relative Operating Characteristics (ROC) type of analysis (Swets & Pickett, 1982). We did this by comparing the distributions of total problem scores in demographically matched referred and nonreferred youths, separately for each sex. (The matched samples are described in Chapter 6.) For each sex, we identified a range of scores where the differences between the cumulative percents of referred and nonreferred youths were greatest. That is, we computed the difference between the cumulative percent of referred youths who obtained all scores up to a particular score and the cumulative percent of nonreferred youths who obtained all scores up to that same score. The score at which the nonreferred youths exceeded the referred youths by the greatest percent represented the most efficient cutpoint, in terms of minimizing the percent of nonreferred youths who scored above the cutpoint ("false positives"), *plus* the percent of referred youths who scored *below* the cutpoint ("false negatives").

The cutpoints for both sexes and all age ranges on the YSR, CBCL, and TRF were compared to determine whether a similar cutpoint and borderline range could provide efficient discrimination for all of them. Scores in the normative samples ranging from about the 82nd to the 90th percentile were found to provide the most efficient discrimination for most sex/age groups on all three instruments. *T* scores of 60 to 63, which span these percentiles, were therefore chosen to demarcate the borderline clinical range.

For categorical discrimination between deviant and nondeviant groups, $T = 60$ serves as the bottom of the clinical range. However, by designating a borderline clinical range, we emphasize that *T* scores from 60 to 63 are less clearly deviant than scores above it. Furthermore, cutpoints other than $T = 60$ may be more effective for particular purposes in particular samples.

SUMMARY

Beside describing youths in terms of specific items, the YSR is designed to identify syndromes of problems. To identify syndromes, we performed principal components/varimax analyses of the YSR problem items scored for clinically referred youths aged 11-18, separately for each sex. Two sets of analyses were performed for each sex/age group. In one set of analyses, all the YSR problem items were included. In the second set, only the 89 items common to the YSR, CBCL, and TRF were included.

Syndromes identified for boys and girls were compared to identify items that were common to a syndrome for both sexes. These items were used to construct a *core syndrome* of items to be scored on the 1991 YSR profile. The version of each core syndrome derived from the 89 common items was compared with analogous core syndromes derived from the CBCL and TRF. Items that were found in the analogous core syndromes from at least two of the three instruments were used to form a *cross-informant syndrome construct.*

The following eight cross-informant syndromes are displayed on the 1991 YSR profile: *Withdrawn, Somatic Complaints, Anxious/Depressed, Social Problems, Thought Problems, Attention Problems, Delinquent Behavior* and *Aggressive Behavior.* An additional syndrome, designated as *Self-Destructive/Identity Problems,* can also be scored from the YSR for boys, but it does not have counterparts for girls on the YSR or for either sex on the CBCL or TRF.

Hand-scored and computer-scored profiles display scores for every problem item, as well as raw scores and T scores for the syndrome scales, Internalizing, Externalizing, and total problem score. Normal, borderline, and clinical ranges are also designated for the scale scores.

Chapter 4
Internalizing and Externalizing
Groupings of Syndromes

As shown in Figure 3-1, the syndrome scales designated as *Withdrawn, Somatic Complaints,* and *Anxious/Depressed* are grouped under the heading *Internalizing.* The syndrome scales designated as *Delinquent Behavior* and *Aggressive Behavior* are grouped under the heading *Externalizing.* These groupings of syndromes reflect a distinction that has been detected in numerous multivariate analyses of children's behavioral/ emotional problems. The two groups of problems have been variously called Personality Problem versus Conduct Problem (Peterson, 1961), Internalizing versus Externalizing (Achenbach, 1966), Inhibition versus Aggression (Miller, 1967), and Overcontrolled versus Undercontrolled (Achenbach & Edelbrock, 1978).

In the pre-1991 profiles, we identified two broad groupings of syndromes that we designated as Internalizing and Externalizing, consistent with the terminology used since the initial multivariate study in this research program (Achenbach, 1966). The pre-1991 groupings were identified by performing second-order principal components analyses of the syndrome scales for each sex/age group on the YSR, CBCL, and TRF. Each group's Internalizing and Externalizing scores were based on their respective set of syndromes. Because the syndrome scales and the items of these scales varied somewhat from one sex/age group and instrument to another, the composition of the Internalizing and Externalizing scores was not uniform.

47

1991 INTERNALIZING AND EXTERNALIZING GROUPINGS

To increase the consistency between the different sex/age groups on the CBCL, YSR, and TRF and between these instruments, we derived the 1991 Internalizing and Externalizing groupings as follows:

1. Using the clinical samples from which our syndrome scales were derived, we computed correlations between the raw scores on the syndrome scales separately for each sex/age group on the YSR, CBCL, and TRF. Items that appear on more than one scale were scored only on the scale for which they had the highest loading.

2. We performed principal factor analyses of the correlations among the scale scores separately for each sex/age group. Principal factor analyses are like principal components analyses except that estimates of communality among the variables are used instead of 1.0 in the principal diagonal. Our choice of factor analysis here was based on new evidence for the superiority of factor analysis in applications to small numbers of variables, such as our eight syndrome scales (Snook & Gorsuch, 1989). Squared multiple correlations among syndrome scale scores were used in the principal diagonal.

3. The two largest factors in each solution were rotated to the varimax criterion. Both rotated factors had eigenvalues >1.0 in all groups.

4. Averaged across all groups on all three instruments, the loadings of the syndrome scales yielded the following rank order of syndromes on the Internalizing factors (mean loadings are in parentheses): 1. Withdrawn (.784); 2. Somatic Complaints (.690); 3. Anxious/

Depressed (.650). The rank order of syndromes on the Externalizing factors was: 1. Aggressive Behavior (.791); 2. Delinquent Behavior (.778).

5. The Internalizing score for each profile is the sum of items on the three Internalizing scales of that profile. The Externalizing score is the sum of items on the two Externalizing scales of that profile. No item is counted twice within either the Internalizing score or the Externalizing score, and no item is included in both an Internalizing and Externalizing scale.

6. Because the composition of some syndrome scales differs among the profiles, there are small differences among the YSR, CBCL, and TRF versions of the Internalizing and Externalizing scores.

Although the Attention Problems scale had moderately high loadings on the various versions of the Externalizing factor, its mean loading of .618 was enough lower than the mean loading of .791 for the Aggressive scale and .778 for the Delinquent scale that it was deemed inappropriate to include with the Externalizing grouping.   The Attention Problems scale is therefore displayed in the middle section of the profiles with the Social Problems and Thought Problems scales, neither of which had consistently high loadings on the Internalizing or Externalizing factors.

Starting on the left side of the profile, the Internalizing scales are listed from left to right in descending order of their rank on the Internalizing factors (Withdrawal, Somatic Complaints, Anxious/Depressed).   On the right side of the profile, the two Externalizing scales are listed from left to right in ascending order of their rank on the Externalizing factors, i. e., Delinquent Behavior, followed by Aggressive Behavior, which is the rightmost scale.

ASSIGNMENT OF INTERNALIZING AND EXTERNALIZING T SCORES

To provide norm referenced scores, we summed the scores obtained on the Internalizing and Externalizing items by the normative samples of each sex/age group on each instrument. The one item that appears on more than one Internalizing scale was counted only once in the Internalizing score. No items of the Delinquent or Aggressive Behavior scales are included on any other syndrome scale.

Percentiles were computed according to the procedure described in Chapter 3. Normalized T scores were assigned in the same manner as described in Chapter 3 for the total problem scores. That is, the T scores were based directly on percentiles up to the 97.7th percentile ($T = 70$). The raw scores ranging from $T = 70$ to the mean of the five highest scores in our clinical samples were then assigned T scores in equal intervals from 71 through 89. The raw scores above the mean of the five highest in our clinical samples were assigned T scores in equal intervals from 90 through 100. Just as with the total problem score, the clinical cutpoint was established at $T = 60$, with the borderline clinical range including T scores of 60 through 63.

To assess a child's problems in terms of the Internalizing and Externalizing groupings, the hand-scored profiles provide guidelines for summing the Internalizing and Externalizing scale scores. Appendix A provides detailed scoring instructions. To the right of the profile, a table is provided for determining the T score equivalent of each Internalizing and Externalizing raw score (see Appendix A for instructions). The computer-scoring programs automatically compute raw scores and T scores for Internalizing and Externalizing.

RELATIONS BETWEEN INTERNALIZING AND EXTERNALIZING SCORES

The Internalizing and Externalizing groupings reflect empirical associations among subsets of scales that involve contrasting kinds of problems. These problems are not mutually exclusive, however, because some individuals may have both kinds of problems. In many samples of children, positive correlations are found between Internalizing and Externalizing scores. Across our normative samples of each sex/age group on each instrument, the mean correlation between Internalizing and Externalizing was .52, computed by Fisher's z transformation. This reflects the fact that children who have very high problem scores in one of the two areas also tend to have at least above-average problem scores in the other area as well. Conversely, children who have very low scores in one area also tend to have relatively low scores in the other area.

Appendix C lists the correlations between YSR Internalizing and Externalizing scores for demographically matched referred and nonreferred samples of each sex in each age range. The mean Pearson r between YSR Internalizing and Externalizing scores was .52 for the referred samples and .64 for the nonreferred samples, computed by z transformation.

Despite the positive association between Internalizing and Externalizing scores found in our samples as a whole, some youths' problems are primarily Internalizing, whereas other youths' problems are primarily Externalizing. This is analogous to the relation between Verbal IQ and Performance IQ on the Wechsler intelligence tests: In most samples, there is a positive correlation between the Wechsler Verbal IQ and Performance IQ (e.g., Wechsler, 1989). Nevertheless, some youths have much higher Verbal than Performance scores or vice versa. Youths who have much higher Verbal than Performance scores may differ in other important ways from those who have much higher Performance than Verbal scores. Similarly, youths who have much higher Internalizing scores than Externalizing scores may differ in other important ways from those who show the opposite pattern. Numerous studies have in fact shown significant differences between subjects classified as having primarily Internalizing versus primarily Externalizing problems (e.g., Achenbach, 1966; Achenbach & Lewis, 1971; Katz, Zigler, & Zalk, 1975; McConaughy, Achenbach, & Gent, 1988; Weintraub, 1973).

Distinguishing Between Internalizing and Externalizing Patterns

Users of the profiles may wish to distinguish between youths whose reported problems are primarily from the Internalizing grouping and those whose problems are primarily from the Externalizing grouping. Such distinctions may be clinically useful for choosing approaches to intervention and for identifying groups of clients with similar problems for purposes such as group therapy, parent training groups, and assignment to residential units. Such distinctions may also be useful for testing hypotheses about differences in etiology, responsiveness to particular treatments, and long-term outcomes.

The specific criteria for distinguishing between youths having primarily Internalizing versus Externalizing problems should be based on the user's aims and the size and nature of the available sample. The criteria chosen for distinguishing between Internalizing and Externalizing patterns will affect the proportion of a sample that can be classified, the homogeneity of the resulting groups, and the associations that may be found between the Internalizing-Externalizing classification and other variables. Very stringent criteria, for example, will severely limit the proportion of youths classified as manifesting Internalizing versus Externalizing patterns. But stringent criteria will also yield relatively extreme groups who are likely to differ more on other variables than would less extreme Internalizing and Externalizing groups.

The trade-offs between stringency of criteria, proportion of youths classified, and degree of association with other variables must be weighed by users of the profiles when choosing criteria for their own purposes. As a general guideline, we suggest that youths not be classified as Internalizing or Externalizing unless (a) their total problem score exceeds the clinical cutpoint on at least one of the three instruments, and (b) the difference between their Internalizing and Externalizing T score is at least 10 points on one instrument or at least 5 points on two instruments. The larger the difference is between T scores and the more consistent the difference is between two or more instruments, the more distinctive the Internalizing and Externalizing groups will be.

SUMMARY

Internalizing and Externalizing groupings of behavioral/ emotional problems were identified by performing second-order factor analyses of the eight 1991 syndrome scales scored separately from each instrument for each sex/age group. The largest two rotated factors in all analyses reflected a distinction between problems of withdrawal, somatic complaints, and anxiety/depression, on the one hand, and delinquent and aggressive behavior, on the other.

On all 1991 profiles, the Internalizing grouping is operationally defined as the sum of scores on the problem items of the Withdrawal, Somatic Complaints, and Anxious/ Depressed scales. The Externalizing grouping is defined as the sum of scores on the problem items of the Delinquent and Aggressive Behavior scales.

The eight scales of the profiles are arranged in order starting with the three Internalizing scales on the left, followed by three scales that did not have consistently high loadings on either the Internalizing or Externalizing factors (Social Problems, Thought Problems, Attention Problems), and ending with the two Externalizing scales on the right. *T* scores were assigned to the Internalizing and Externalizing scores in the same way as was done for the total problem scores.

The relation between Internalizing and Externalizing scores is analogous to the relation between verbal and performance IQ scores on intelligence tests. Although Internalizing and Externalizing scores represent contrasting kinds of problems, they are not mutually exclusive. Across groups, Internalizing scores typically correlate positively with Externalizing scores, because individuals who have very high scores in one area tend to have at least above-average scores in the other area as well. Nevertheless, youths who have much higher Internalizing than Externalizing scores may differ in important ways from youths who show the reverse pattern. Guidelines were provided for distinguishing between youths whose problems are primarily in the Internalizing area and those whose problems are primarily in the Externalizing area.

Chapter 5
Test-Retest Reliability and Stability

Reliability refers to agreement between repeated assessments when the phenomena being assessed are expected to remain constant. Because the YSR is designed to obtain adolescents' self-reports about their own functioning, the main way to assess reliability is to compare YSR responses on two occasions across an interval long enough to avoid much recall but short enough to avoid major changes in the target phenomena. We assessed reliability by asking 50 youths in a general population sample to complete the YSR twice at intervals averaging 7 days. We analyzed the relations between Time 1 and Time 2 scores in two ways: *(a)* Pearson correlations, symbolized by *r*, which mainly reflect similarities in *rank ordering* between the two sets of scores; and *(b)* *t* tests, which reflect differences between the *mean magnitudes* of the two sets of scores.

Because Pearson *r* reflects similarities between the rank orders of scores at Time 1 and Time 2, it is high if self-ratings by individual youths retain approximately the same rank compared to those of other youths in the sample. Because it is not determined by the absolute magnitude of scores, *r* can be high even if all the Time 1 scores differ in magnitude from all the Time 2 scores. The *t* test, by contrast, indicates the magnitude of the differences between the sets of scores relative to their variance. A *t* test could therefore show that there is no significant difference between Time 1 and Time 2 scores, even though a low *r* indicates that individuals have changed their ranks from Time 1 to Time 2. By reporting both the *r* and the results of the *t* test for Time 1 versus Time 2 scores, we enable the reader to consider consistency separately for rank order and

55

for the magnitude of scores. Furthermore, because reliabilities may differ according to the sex and age of the youths, we computed them separately for each sex and also for ages 11-14 versus 15-18. (The sample was not large enough to provide adequate subsamples divided simultaneously by sex and age.)

Table 5-1 presents the 7-day test-retest r for raw scores on each scale computed separately for boys and girls and for ages 11-14 versus 15-18. It also presents rs for all youths combined for all scales except Self-Destructive/Identity Problems, which exists only for boys.

As Table 5-1 shows, all rs were significant at $p < .05$, except the Activities scale for boys and the Thought Problems scale for 11- to 14-year-olds, which were both $r = .37$, $p < .10$. The test-retest rs tended to be somewhat higher for girls than boys. Considering only the rs that were for separate scales rather than being based on multiple scales, 7 were higher for girls, while 3 were higher for boys, which is not a significant difference by sign test. The age differences were more consistent, however, as 10 of the 11 independent scale rs (including Self-Destructive/Identity Problems) were higher for older than younger youths ($p = .012$ by sign test). The test-retest rs for total competence and total problems were also considerably higher for the older than younger youths, being .87 versus .69 for total competence and .91 versus .70 for total problems, although the Ns were too small for these differences in correlations to be significant. The higher test-retest reliability among older youths is consistent with the age trend found on the Diagnostic Interview Schedule for Children (DISC), where test-retest intraclass correlations averaged .71 for 14- to 18-year-olds versus .60 for 10- to 13-year-olds (Edelbrock, Costello, Dulcan, Kalas, & Conover, 1985). The test-retest r = .91 for YSR total problems among the 15- to 18-year-olds was similar to the test-retest r = .93 for CBCL total problems and r = .86 for TRF total problems over one-week periods (Achenbach, 1991b; Achenbach & Edelbrock, 1986). YSR total problem ratings by 15- to 18-year-olds were thus as

Table 5-1
One-Week Test-Retest Reliabilities of YSR scales

Scale	Boys	Girls	Age 11-14	Age 15-18	Combined
N =	22	28	26	24	50
Activities	(.37)	.85	.56	.74	.67
Social	.80	.79	.76[a]	.83	.80[ab]
Total Competence	.74	.84	.69	.87	.80
Mean r	.67	.83	.68	.82	.76
Withdrawn	.60	.76	.59	.78	.70[ab]
Somatic Complaints	.78	.61	.72	.49	.65
Anxious/Depressed	.74	.87[a]	.67[ab]	.93	.81[a]
Social Problems	.50	.65	.40	.77	.57
Thought Problems	.45	.68[ab]	(.37)	.67	.47
Attention Problems	.62	.90	.75	.81	.79
Delinquent Behavior	.62	.83	.47	.88	.72
Aggressive Behavior	.83	.77[a]	.78	.87	.79[a]
Self Dest/Ident Problems	.64	---	.67	.69	.64
Internalizing	.76	.85[a]	.67	.91	.80[ab]
Externalizing	.80	.84[ab]	.76	.91	.81[ab]
Total Problems	.78	.86[a]	.70	.91[ab]	.79[a]
Mean r	.69	.77	.65	.83[ab]	.72

Note. All Pearson *r*s were significant at *p* <.05 except those in parentheses.
[a]Time 1 > Time 2, *p* <.05, by *t* test.
[b]When corrected for the number of comparisons, Time 1 vs. Time 2 difference was not significant.

reliable as CBCL and TRF total problem ratings by parents and teachers, although YSR ratings by 11- to 14-year-olds were less reliable.

There was a tendency for scores to decline from the first rating to the second on some scales. This tendency was nominally significant at *p* <.05 by *t* test in 17 of the 84 comparisons, as shown by superscript *a* in Table 5-1. Superscript *b* indicates the 9 of the 17 differences most likely to be significant by chance because they had the smallest *t* values (Sakoda, Cohen, & Beall, 1954). The magnitude of decline in scores from Time 1 to Time 2 was generally small, with the mean decline being 0.8 points. A similar tendency, called a "practice effect," has been found in ratings by parents (Achenbach, 1991b; Miller, Hampe, Barrett, & Noble, 1972) and teachers (Evans, 1975; Milich, Roberts, Loney, & Caputo, 1980), as well as in psychiatric interviews with adolescents (Edelbrock et al., 1985) and adults (Robins, 1985).

LONGER-TERM STABILITY
OF YSR SCALES

Table 5-2 presents Pearson rs for self-ratings by a general population sample of 11- to 14-year-old students who completed the YSR on two occasions averaging 7 months apart. The correlations are presented for each sex separately for ages 11-12 and 13-14, and for the entire group combined. Although rs for older youths were higher than for younger youths on all the competence scales, the age differences in correlations for the problem scales ran in both directions. As a result, there was no significant tendency for one age group to have higher stability correlations than the other age group. Age differences may have been found, however, if groups differing more in age were tested, as was done for the 7-day test-retest reliabilities shown in Table 5-1. In a clinical sample of 12- to 17-year-olds, the stability r for the total problem score was .69 over a mean interval of 6 months (Achenbach & Edelbrock, 1983).

According to t tests, 5 of the 84 comparisons showed nominally significant differences ($p < .05$) between the YSR scores obtained at the beginning and end of the 7-month interval. As this is fewer than the 9 differences expected by chance, they are not indicated in Table 5-2.

Table 5-2
Seven-Month Test-Retest Stabilities of YSR Scales

Scale	Boys	Girls	Age 11-12	Age 13-14	Combined
N =	49	62	83	28	111
Activities	.43	.25	.38	.47	.39
Social	.44	.49	.43	.60	.47
Total Competence	.69	.51	.57	.87	.62
Mean r	.53	.42	.46	.69	.50
Withdrawn	(.11)	.36	.28	.39	.30
Somatic Complaints	.42	.51	.53	(.28)	.47
Anxious/Depressed	.36	.71	.62	.48	.60
Social Problems	(.26)	.55	.42	.69	.45
Thought Problems	.60	.57	.56	.66	.58
Attention Problems	.61	.56	.62	.52	.59
Delinquent Behavior	.35	.59	.56	(.27)	.48
Aggressive Behavior	.47	.46	.48	.46	.48
Self Dest/Ident Problems	.31	---	.44	(.07)	.31
Internalizing	.35	.60	.53	.50	.52
Externalizing	.45	.51	.52	.43	.49
Total Problems	.45	.64	.58	.57	.56
Mean r	.40	.52	.52	.46	.49

Note. All Pearson *r*s were significant at $p < .05$ except those in parentheses. Five comparisons showed significant decreases in mean scores, which is fewer than the 9 expected by chance. (From B.E. Compas, D.C. Howell, V.S. Phares, & R. Williams, unpublished data.)

INTERNAL CONSISTENCY

A property of scales that is sometimes referred to as "reliability" is their internal consistency. This is the correlation between half of a scale's items and the other half of its items. Although internal consistency is called "split-half reliability," it cannot tell us the degree to which a scale will produce the same results over different occasions when the target phenomena are expected to remain constant. Furthermore, scales with relatively low internal consistency may be more *valid* than scales with very high internal consistency. For example, if a scale consists of 25 repetitions of exactly the same item, it should produce very high internal consistency, because respondents should repeatedly score the same item in the same way on a particular occasion. However, such a scale would usually be less valid than a scale that uses 25 different items to assess the same phenomenon. Because each of the 25 different items is likely to tap different aspects of the target phenomenon and to be subject to different errors of measurement, the 25 different items are likely to provide better measurement despite lower internal consistency than a scale that repeats the same item 25 times.

Our syndrome scales were derived from principal components analyses of the correlations among items. The composition of the scales is therefore based on internal consistency among certain subsets of items. Measures of the internal consistency of these scales are thus redundant. Nevertheless, because some users may wish to know how internally consistent our scales are, Cronbach's (1951) *alpha* is displayed in Appendix B for each scale. *Alpha* represents the mean of the correlations between all possible sets of half the items comprising a scale. *Alpha* tends to be directly related to the length of the scale, because half the items of a short scale provide a less stable measure than half the items of a long scale. The *alphas* for our scales having few items therefore tend to be lower than for our scales having many items.

SUMMARY

For raw scores on the YSR competence scales, the mean 7-day test-retest reliability was $r = .68$ for 11- to 14-year-olds and $r = .82$ for 15- to 18-year-olds. For the problem scales, the mean rs were .65 for 11- to 14-year-olds and .83 for 15- to 18-year-olds. The mean change in scores was 0.8 over the 7-day period. On the total problem score, the test-retest *r* was .70 for 11- to 14-year-olds and .91 for 15- to 18-year-olds. The latter is comparable to test-retest *r*s obtained for parent- and teacher-ratings of total problems.

Over a 7-month period, the mean stability *r* was .50 for competence scales and .49 for problem scales in a general population sample of 11- to 14-year-olds. Stability *r*s were .62 for total competence and .56 for total problems. In a clinical sample of 12- to 17-year-olds, the 6-month stability *r* was .69 for the total problem score.

Chapter 6
Validity

Validity concerns the accuracy with which a procedure measures what it is supposed to measure. The YSR is designed to obtain adolescents' reports of their own problems and competencies in a standardized format. Like other procedures for assessing behavioral/emotional problems and competencies, the validity of the YSR must be evaluated in relation to a variety of criteria, none of which is definitive by itself.

Our Manuals for the CBCL and TRF (Achenbach, 1991b, c) provide evidence of construct validity for CBCL and TRF syndromes in terms of significant correlations with syndrome scales derived from other instruments. However, the lack of instruments resembling the YSR currently limits the possibilities for testing construct validity in this way. It is our hope that the availability of the YSR will encourage further research on syndromes identified via adolescent self-reports as one avenue for testing construct validity. In the meantime, the *Integrative Guide for the 1991 CBCL/4-18, YSR, and TRF Profiles* (Achenbach, 1991a) presents a variety of analyses on relations between scores obtained from the YSR, CBCL, and TRF, while Chapter 11 presents correlations between YSR and CBCL scales separately for youths and parents of each sex. The different perspectives of adolescents and their parents, however, limit the potential for testing construct validity via correlations of this sort. In this chapter, we will present findings on the content validity of YSR items and the criterion-related validity of YSR scale scores.

CONTENT VALIDITY OF YSR ITEMS

Content validity refers to whether an instrument's content includes what it is intended to measure. The YSR items are based on CBCL items that were developed to describe competencies and problems that are of concern to parents and mental health workers. The CBCL items were derived from earlier research on child/adolescent psychiatric case histories (Achenbach, 1966), the clinical and research literature, and consultation with clinical and developmental psychologists, psychiatrists, and social workers. Pilot editions of the CBCL were tested with parents in several clinics and were revised on the basis of feedback from parents, paraprofessionals, and clinicians.

After finalizing the CBCL items, we compared the item scores obtained by clinically referred and nonreferred children and youths (N = 2,600 in our 1976 samples; Achenbach & Edelbrock, 1981). On all but two of the CBCL problem items (*Allergy* and *Asthma*), the referred sample obtained significantly (p <.005) higher scores than the nonreferred sample. Except for *Allergy* and *Asthma*, the CBCL problem items were thus significantly associated with referrals for mental health services that had been made independently of CBCL scores.

In our 1989 CBCL samples, nearly all the CBCL problem items again discriminated significantly between referred and nonreferred children (Achenbach, 1991b). Because *Allergy* and *Asthma* again failed to discriminate significantly on the CBCL and also failed to discriminate between referred and nonreferred youths on the YSR, these items are now omitted from the CBCL and YSR problem scores.

As shown in Figures 1-1 and 1-2, 17 competence items and 102 problem items, plus an open-ended item for other physical problems, were adapted to the YSR from the CBCL. The CBCL items deemed inappropriate for the YSR included three competence items concerning special class placement, grade repetition, and other school problems, plus 16 problem items, such as CBCL Item *98. Thumb-sucking*, which are at too young a level or are seldom acknowledged by adolescents. The 16 omitted problem items were replaced with socially desirable items that encourage respondents to report something favorable about themselves, as indicated in Figure 1-2.

To test the associations between YSR responses and referral for mental health services, we compared the scores obtained on every item by 1,054 youths referred for mental health services and 1,054 demographically similar nonreferred youths drawn from the 1989 normative sample described in Chapter 2. The nonreferred and referred samples were matched as closely as possible for SES and ethnicity. On Hollingshead's (1975) 9-step scale for parental occupation, the mean SES was 5.4 (SD = 2.2) for the nonreferred sample and 5.2 (SD = 2.4) for the referred sample. Ethnicity was 79% white, 18% black, and 3% mixed or other for the referred sample, compared to 73% white, 18% black, and 9% mixed or other for the nonreferred sample.

As detailed in Chapter 7, the referred youths scored themselves significantly higher (p <.01) on 95 of the 101 problem items that are now counted toward the total problem score (after excluding *Allergy* and *Asthma*). Referred youths also scored significantly lower than nonreferred youths on 14 of the 17 competence items, but higher on 2 of the 17. These two items refer to the number of sports and number of non-sports recreational activities, which are omitted from the 1991 competence scale scores. As discussed in Chapter 7, there is evidence from other research that disturbed youngsters tend to rate themselves more favorably than normal youngsters on activities (Zimet & Farley, 1987) and more favorably than adults rate them (Kazdin, French, & Unis, 1983; Piers, 1972; Zimet & Farley, 1986).

CRITERION-RELATED VALIDITY
OF YSR SCALES

One of the main reasons for empirically deriving syndromes was the lack of a satisfactory taxonomy of child and adolescent disorders. Although recent editions of the DSM have increased the precision of diagnostic criteria (American Psychiatric Association, 1980, 1987), the DSM's diagnostic categories have not been derived from assessment of children and adolescents.

There are similarities and statistical associations between several DSM categories and the syndromes that we have derived empirically from the YSR (Weinstein, Noam, Grimes, Stone, & Schwab-Stone, 1990), as well as from the CBCL (Edelbrock & Costello, 1988) and the TRF (Edelbrock, Costello, & Kessler, 1984). Nevertheless, the current DSM categories have not been adequately validated, nor are they operationally defined according to any particular assessment procedures. In lieu of better validated diagnostic criteria, we have used actual referral for mental health services to test the criterion-related validity of our empirically derived scales.

We recognize that referral for mental health services is not an infallible criterion of need for help. Some youths in our referred sample may not have needed professional help, whereas some in our nonreferred sample may have needed help. Yet, as detailed elsewhere (Achenbach & Edelbrock, 1981), actual referral seemed as ecologically valid as any other practical alternative for large representative samples.

Using YSRs for the 1,054 nonreferred and 1,054 referred youths described earlier, we did separate analyses for the 1,072 boys and 1,036 girls from these samples. To assess the effects of referral status and the demographic variables, we computed multiple regressions of scale scores on referral status (scored 0 for nonreferred, 1 for referred), age, SES (Hollingshead 9-step scale for parental occupation), and ethnicity, which was analyzed via dummy variables coded as white = 1, nonwhite =

0, and black = 1, nonblack = 0. There were not enough subjects of any one other ethnic group to warrant entry as a separate independent variable.

To take account of possible chance effects occurring in these analyses, we have marked (superscript f) the number of nominally significant effects that could have arisen by chance in the analyses of each independent variable within each sex. In view of our large Ns, we used a .01 *alpha* level and a .01 protection level for determining the number of significant findings apt to occur by chance (Sakoda et al., 1954). The effects marked with superscript f are the nominally significant effects that had the smallest F values, which are assumed to be the effects most likely to be significant by chance.

Table 6-1 shows the effect size for each variable in terms of the semipartial r^2 obtained after partialling out any other independent variables that accounted for more variance in the scale score. According to Cohen's (1988) criteria for effect sizes when other independent variables are partialled out via multiple regression, effects accounting for 2 to 13% of variance in the dependent variable are considered small; effects accounting for 13 to 26% of variance are medium; and effects accounting for $\geq 26\%$ of variance are large.

Referral Status Differences Between Scale Scores

As shown in Table 6-1, all effects of referral status that were significant at $p < .01$ reflected higher competence scores and lower problem scores for nonreferred than referred youths. The one effect of referral status that did not reach $p < .01$ was nevertheless significant at $p < .015$, reflecting higher scores for nonreferred than referred boys on the Activities scale, accounting for 2% of the variance.

For those scales that are scored for both sexes, the differences between referred and nonreferred youths accounted for more variance among girls than among boys, with the exception of the Social Problems syndrome, where referral status

Table 6-1
Percent of Variance Accounted for by Significant ($p < .01$)
Effects of Referral Status, Age, SES, and Ethnicity
in YSR Scale Scores for Matched Referred and Nonreferred Samples

	1,072 Boys				1,036 Girls			
	Ref Stat[a]	Age[b]	SES[c]	Black[d]	Ref Stat[a]	Age[b]	SES[c]	Black[d]
Competence Scales								
Activities	--	$<1^{Yf}$	--	--	2^f	$<1^{Yf}$	1^f	--
Social	6	--	--	--	10	--	3^f	$<1^N$
Total Competence	5^f	--	$<1^f$	--	9	--	3	1^N
Problem Scales								
Withdrawn	8	--	--	--	13	$<1^O$	--	$<1^{Bf}$
Somatic Complaints	5^f	1^{Yf}	--	--	9	--	--	--
Anxious/Depressed	8	--	--	$<1^N$	13	$<1^{Of}$	--	$<1^{Nf}$
Social Problems	8	2^Y	<1	--	8	1^Y	--	--
Thought Probs	6	--	1	--	7^f	--	--	--
Attention Probs	8	--	--	3^N	11	--	--	1^N
Delinquent Behav	12	3°	--	$<1^N$	19	2^O	--	--
Aggressive Behav	7	--	--	1^N	12	--	--	--
Self-Destructive[e]	10	--	--	$<1^{Nf}$	Not scored for girls			
Internalizing	9	--	--	--	15	--	--	--
Externalizing	10	--	--	1^N	17	--	--	--
Total Problems	13	--	$<1^f$	$<1^{Nf}$	18	--	--	--

Note. Analyses were multiple regressions of raw scale scores on referral status, age, SES, white vs. nonwhite, and black vs. nonblack. The percent of variance accounted for by each independent variable is represented by the semipartial r^2 for that variable after partialling out the effects of variables accounting for more variance.
[a]All competence scores were higher and problem scores were lower for nonreferred than referred youths. [b]O = older scored higher; Y = younger scored higher. [c]All significant SES effects reflected higher competence and lower problem scores for upper than lower SES. [d]B = blacks scored higher; N = nonblacks scored higher; effects of white vs. nonwhite ethnicity are not displayed because they were fewer than expected by chance. [e]Self-Destructive/Identity Problems scale not scored for girls. [f]Not significant when corrected for number of analyses.

accounted for 8% of the variance in scores for both sexes, and the Activities Scale, where referral status accounted for 2% of the variance for both sexes. Self-reports by adolescent girls were thus more strongly associated with referral for mental health services than were self-reports by adolescent boys in nearly all areas tapped by the YSR.

The largest effects of referral status were 19% for Delinquent Behavior, 18% for total problems, 17% for Externalizing, and 15% for Internalizing, all among girls. Referral status accounted for 13% of the variance in the girls' scores on the Withdrawn and Anxious/Depressed scales, and in the total problem score for the boys. Referral status had its smallest effects on the Activities scale, accounting for 2% of the variance for both sexes. Among the syndrome scales, the smallest association with referral status was found for Somatic Complaints among the boys (5% of variance) and Thought Problems among the girls (7% of variance).

Demographic Differences Between Scale Scores

There were no significant effects of white versus nonwhite ethnicity for boys. The two effects of this variable found for girls were no more than expected by chance. The effects of white versus nonwhite ethnicity are therefore omitted from Table 6-1.

As Table 6-1 shows, all the significant effects of age, SES, and black versus nonblack ethnicity fell either at the very low end of the 2 to 13% range defined by Cohen as small or below this range. Age effects ran in both directions, with younger youths obtaining higher scores on some scales and older youths obtaining higher scores on other scales. The largest age effects were on the Delinquent Behavior scale, where older youths of both sexes tended to obtain higher scores (3% of variance for boys, 2% for girls). The exact shape of the age effects can be seen in Figure 6-1, which shows the mean of the raw scale

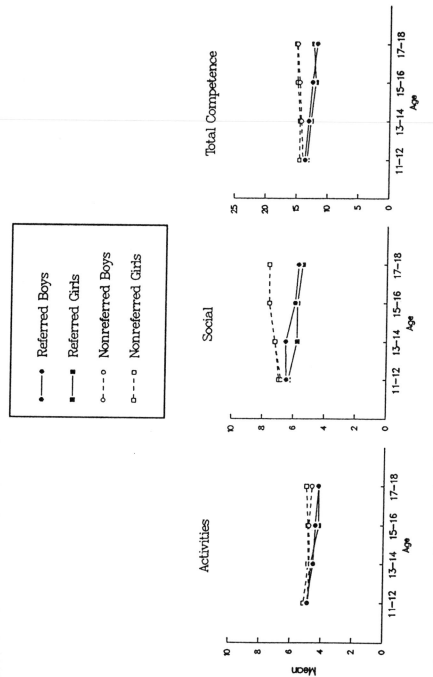

Figure 6-1. Mean YSR scale scores for demographically matched referred and nonreferred samples that were used in regression analyses.

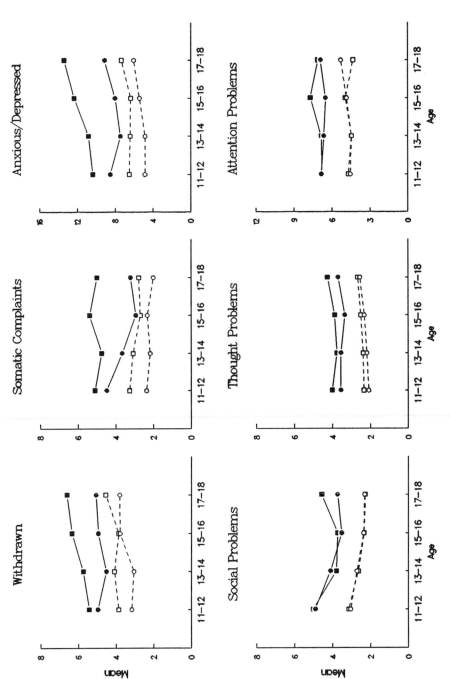

Figure 6-1 (cont.) Mean YSR scale scores for demographically matched referred and nonreferred samples that were used in regression analyses.

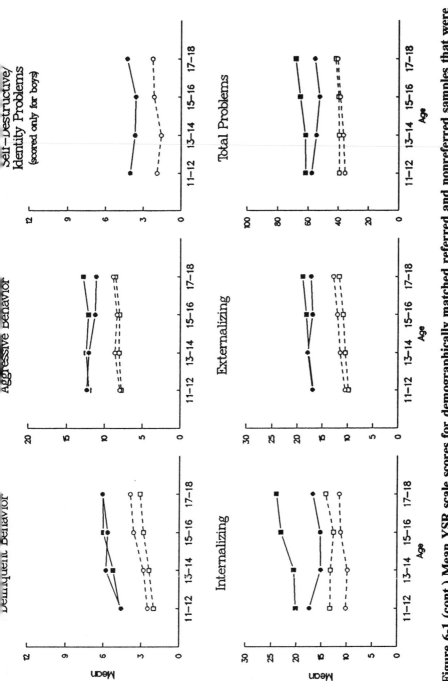

Figure 6-1 (cont.) Mean YSR scale scores for demographically matched referred and nonreferred samples that were used in regression analyses.

scores obtained by referred and nonreferred youths of each sex from age 11 to 18.

All significant SES effects reflected higher competence scores and lower problem scores for upper than for lower SES youths. The only SES effects that accounted for >1% of variance were the 3% effects on girls' self-ratings of the Social and total competence scores.

All the significant effects of black versus nonblack ethnicity among boys reflected higher problem scores for nonblacks than for blacks, with the largest effect accounting for 3% of the variance in the Attention Problems scale. Among girls, nonblacks scored themselves higher on the Social, total competence, Anxious/Depressed, and Thought Problems scale, whereas blacks scored themselves higher on the Withdrawn scale. However, none of these effects accounted for >1% of the variance.

CLASSIFICATION OF YOUTHS
ACCORDING TO CLINICAL CUTPOINTS

The regression analyses reported in the previous section showed that all quantitative scale scores significantly discriminated between referred and nonreferred youths after partialling out the effects of demographic variables. Beside the quantitative scores, each scale has cutpoints for distinguishing categorically between the normal and clinical range. The choice of cutpoints for the different scales was discussed in Chapters 2, 3, and 4.

For some clinical and research purposes, users may wish to distinguish between youths who are in the normal versus clinical range according to the cutpoints. Because categorical distinctions are usually least reliable for individuals who score close to the border of a category, we have identified a borderline clinical range for each scale. The addition of a borderline category often yields stronger associations between clinical status and classification of children according to their scale scores. This was demonstrated by phi correlations computed in our matched samples for the association between clinical status and scores trichotomized into the normal, borderline clinical, and clinical ranges versus phi correlations for scores dichotomized into the normal and clinical range, with borderline scores included in the clinical range. In virtually all comparisons on all scales for each sex, the inclusion of the borderline range yielded higher phi correlations than did the dichotomous classification into the normal versus clinical range. Inclusion of the borderline category also yielded higher phi correlations for agreement between scores obtained from pairs of informants, including mother versus father, parent versus teacher, parent versus youth, and teacher versus youth (Achenbach, 1991a).

Despite the greater statistical power generally afforded by continuous quantitative scores and even by inclusion of a borderline range, users may wish to distinguish categorically between the normal and clinical range. The following sections report findings that indicate the degree to which classification of YSR scale scores as normal versus clinical distinguish between demographically matched nonreferred versus referred youths.

Odds Ratios

One approach to analyzing associations between categorical classifications is by computing *relative risk odds ratios* (Fleiss, 1981), which are used in epidemiological research. The odds ratio indicates the odds that people who have a particular risk factor will also manifest a particular outcome, relative to the odds that people lacking the risk factor will manifest the outcome. The comparison between outcome rates for those who do and do not have the risk factor is expressed as the ratio of the odds of having the outcome if the risk factor is present, to the odds of having the outcome if the risk factor is absent.

For example, a study of relations between smoking (a risk factor) and lung cancer (an outcome) may yield a relative risk odds ratio of 5.5. This means that people who smoke have 5.5 times greater odds of developing lung cancer than people who do not smoke.

We applied odds ratio analyses to the relations between YSR scores and referral status as follows: For each YSR scale, we first classified youths from our matched nonreferred and referred samples according to whether they scored in the normal range or in the clinical range (including the borderline clinical range). Scoring in the clinical range on the YSR was thus equivalent to a "risk factor" in epidemiological research. We then computed the odds that youths who scored in the clinical range on a particular scale were from the referred sample, relative to the odds for youths who scored in the normal range. (Because referred youths were already referred at the time they completed the YSR, we could also have made referral status the "risk factor" and YSR scores the "outcome variable." However, because we used odds ratios to indicate the strength of the contemporaneous association between YSR scores and referral status, rather than a predictive relation between a risk factor and a later outcome, the choice of the risk factor was not important and did not affect the obtained odds ratios.)

The relative risk odds ratio is a nonparametric statistic computed from a 2 x 2 table. We therefore included both sexes in the same analysis to provide a summary odds ratio across all subjects. The statistical significance of the odds ratio is evaluated by computing confidence intervals.

Table 6-2 summarizes the odds ratios for relations between scale scores in the clinical range and referral status. Table 6-2 also shows the percent of referred and nonreferred youths who scored in the clinical range according to cutpoints on the scales. Confidence intervals showed that all the odds ratios were significantly greater than 1.0, while chi squares showed that the differences between referred and nonreferred youths scoring in

Table 6-2
Odds Ratios and Percent of Referred and
Nonreferred Samples Scoring in the YSR Clinical Range

Scale	Odds ratio	Percent in Clinical Range	
		Referred	Nonreferred
Activities	2.1	9	5
Social	5.3	18	4
Total Competence	2.9	38	17
Withdrawn	3.9	16	5
Somatic Complaints	3.9	19	6
Anxious/Depressed	4.8	23	6
Social Problems	4.5	22	6
Thought Problems	4.2	19	5
Attention Problems	4.7	24	6
Delinquent Behavior	6.4	29	6
Aggressive Behavior	5.0	23	6
Self-Destructive/			
Identity Problems (boys only)	3.8	18	5
Internalizing	3.9	45	18
Externalizing	4.3	45	16
Total Problems	5.0	53	19
≥ 1 Syndrome in Clinical Range	5.6	62	23
Int and/or Ext in Clinical Range	4.4	61	26
Total Comp and/or Probs in			
Clinical Range	4.8	70	33

Note. Total N = 1,054 referred and 1,054 demographically matched nonreferred, except Competence (N = 1,720) and Self-Destructive/Identity Problems (N = 1,072). In all analyses, the proportion of referred scoring in the clinical range was significantly greater than the proportion of nonreferred at p <.01 according to confidence intervals for odds ratios and chi squares for 2 x 2 tables.

the clinical range were significant in all comparisons ($p < .01$). The largest odds ratios were for Delinquent Behavior (odds ratio = 6.4), having ≥ 1 syndrome in the clinical range (5.6), and the Social scale (5.3).

Combined Competence and Problem Scores

Each competence and syndrome score reflects deviance in a particular area that may characterize only a small proportion of referred youths. The total competence and total problem scores, on the other hand, tap the full range of functioning assessed by the YSR. The lower clinical cutpoints for these scores automatically classify larger percents of both the referred and nonreferred samples as being in the clinical range than do the higher cutpoints of the more specific competence and syndrome scales. As Table 6-2 shows, 38% of referred youths scored in the clinical range on the total competence score and 53% on the total problem score. This compares with 17% of the nonreferred youths scoring in the clinical range on the total competence score and 19% on the total problem score.

When the cutpoints for the total competence and problem scores were combined by classifying youths as clinical if they were deviant on either or both scores, 70% of the referred sample and 33% of the nonreferred sample were classified as clinical, as shown in Table 6-2. Combining the 30% of referred youths classified as normal (false negatives) and the 33% of normal youths classified as clinical (false positives) yields an overall misclassification rate of 30% + 33%/2 = 31.5%.

The combination of the total competence and problem scores can be used to create a borderline range that takes account of both measures. This can be done by classifying youths into the following four categories: (a) normal range on both the total competence and total problem scores; (b) clinical range on the competence score but normal on the problem score; (c) normal on the competence score but clinical on the problem score; *(d)* clinical on both scores. When category *a* was defined as normal, categories *b* and *c* as borderline, and category *d* as clinical, 30.1% of the referred youths were classified as normal (false negatives), while 3.2% of the nonreferred youths were classified as clinical (false positives). (These percents were obtained by computing the percents of false negatives and false positives separately for each sex and then taking their unweighted mean.)

Combining the false negatives obtained in the referred samples with the false positives obtained in the nonreferred samples produced an overall misclassification rate of 16.6%, with 38.5% classified as borderline. The borderline group could be reduced to 14.7% by combining category *c* (deviant only on the total problem score) with category *d* (deviant on both the competence and problem scores). However, this increased the false positive rate to 18.5%, for an overall misclassification rate of 24.3%.

Because it is seldom warranted to make a definitive clinical versus nonclinical judgment for every case on the basis of any single procedure, it is prudent to allow a borderline group. Thus, the combination of total competence and total problem scores can yield a good overall misclassification rate of 16.6% (30.1% false positives and 3.2% false negatives), as judged by our criterion of referral status, if a 38.5% borderline group is allowed. This borderline group can be reduced to 14.7% by including only youths who are in the normal range on the total problem score but deviant on the total competence score, yielding an overall misclassification rate of 24.3%.

Discriminant Analyses

The foregoing sections dealt with use of unweighted combinations of total competence and problem scores to discriminate between youths who were referred for help with behavioral/emotional problems versus youths who were not referred. It is possible that weighted combinations of total scores, scales, or items might produce better discrimination. To test this possibility, we performed discriminant analyses in which the criterion groups were the demographically matched referred and nonreferred youths. Separate discriminant analyses were performed for the 1,072 matched boys and 1,036 matched girls.

The following three sets of discriminant analyses were performed for each sex: *(a)* the total competence and problem scores were used as predictors; *(b)* the two competence scales and all the syndrome scales (including Self-Destructive/Identity Problems for boys) were used as candidate predictors from which significant predictors were selected; *(c)* all the competence and problem items were used as candidate predictors from which significant predictors were selected.

Discriminant analyses selectively weight predictors to maximize their collective associations with the particular criterion groups being analyzed. The weighting process makes use of characteristics of the sample that may differ from other samples. To avoid overestimating the accuracy of the classification obtained by discriminant analyses, it is therefore necessary to correct for the "shrinkage" in associations that would occur when discriminant weights derived in one sample are applied in a new sample. To correct for shrinkage, we employed a "jackknife" procedure whereby the discriminant function for each sample was computed multiple times with a different subject held out of the sample each time (SAS Institute, 1988). The discriminant function was then cross-validated multiple times by testing the accuracy of its prediction for each of the "hold-out" subjects. Finally, the percentage of correct predictions was averaged across all the hold-out subjects. It is these cross-validated predictions that we will present.

Total Competence and Problem Scores. Averaged across boys and girls, the mean misclassification rate was 28.1%, with the percent of false negatives (referred youths classified as normal) being more than 2.5 times as great as the false positives. The mean misclassification rate of 28.1% was only somewhat better than the mean misclassification rate of 31.5% obtained by classifying youths as normal if both their (unweighted) total competence and problem scores were in the normal range and as clinical if one or both scores were in the clinical range. However, it was not as good as the 16.6% misclassification rate obtained by allowing 38.5% borderline cases who were normal on one score but not the other.

Scale Scores. When the two competence scales and all the syndrome scales were tested as candidate predictors, four scales were retained as making significant ($p < .05$) independent contributions for each sex. Of the competence scales, the Social scale was a significant predictor of referral status for each sex. Of the syndrome scales, the Delinquent Behavior scale was the strongest predictor for both sexes. The remaining predictors for boys were the Social Problems and Self-Destructive/Identity Problems scales. For girls, the remaining predictors were the Withdrawn and Somatic Complaints scales. The total misclassification rate was 28.1%, the same as when the total competence and problem scores were the predictors in discriminant analyses.

Item Scores. When all competence and problem items were tested as candidate predictors, from 15 to 18 problem items and from 5 to 6 competence items were retained as significant predictors. The mean misclassification rate was 21.4%, which is better than the 28.1% rates obtained by using weighted combinations of total scores or scale scores. The competence items that were significant for both sexes included: number of jobs, getting along with others, and academic performance. The problem items that were significant for both sexes included: *25. I don't get along with other kids; 67. I run away from home;* and *81. I steal at home.* These items thus have especially strong associations with referral status, even when taken in combination with all other items. Item 67 also showed one of the strongest associations with referral status in the analyses of covariance (ANCOVAs) reported in Chapter 7. Item *103. I am unhappy, sad, or depressed* showed the strongest association with referral status in the discriminant analysis for girls and in the ANCOVAs of the YSR items. It was among the three strongest predictors of referral status in discriminant analyses of all four sex/age groups on the CBCL, as well as having the strongest association with referral status in the ANCOVAs of CBCL items (Achenbach, 1991b). It also had some of the strongest associations with referral status in TRF ratings (Achenbach, 1991c). Whether based on self-reports, parents' reports, or teachers' reports, the dysphoric affect tapped by this item is thus an exceptionally strong sign of clinically significant deviance, although in self-reports it appears to be a stronger sign for girls than boys.

PROBABILITY OF PARTICULAR TOTAL SCORES BEING FROM THE REFERRED VERSUS NONREFERRED SAMPLES

To provide a further picture of relations between particular scores and referral status, Table 6-3 displays the probability of particular total competence and problem T scores being from our referred samples. The probabilities were determined by tabulating the proportion of youths from our matched referred and nonreferred samples who had scores within each of the intervals shown. T scores were used to provide a uniform metric for both sexes. Because T scores for the total competence and problem scores were not truncated, they are highly correlated with the raw scores.

As can be seen from Table 6-3, the probability that a competence score was from the referred sample *decreased* fairly steadily as the magnitude of the competence scores increased. Conversely, the probability that a total problem

Table 6-3
Probability of YSR Total Competence and Total Problems
T Score Being from Referred Sample

Total Competence	Boys	Girls	Total Problems	Boys	Girls
N^a =	875	845	N =	1,072	1,036
0 - 24	.86	.86	0 - 35	.27	.11
25 - 28	.71	.95	36 - 39	.31	.22
29 - 32	.76	.56	40 - 43	.30	.23
33 - 36	.55	.57	44 - 47	.38	.33
37 - 40[b]	.41	.59	48 - 51	.37	.35
41 - 44	.51	.44	52 - 55	.45	.48
45 - 48	.40	.48	56 - 59	.43	.42
49 - 52	.25	.32	60[c]- 63	.67	.63
53 - 56	.33	.32	64 - 67	.69	.69
57 - 60	.22	.19	68 - 71	.78	.84
61 - 64	.36	.14	72 - 75	.88	.93
65 - 80	.34	.29	76 -100	.93	.86

Note. Samples were demographically matched referred and nonreferred youths
[a]*N*s for total competence scores are smaller than for total problem scores due to missing competence data, e.g., for subjects not attending school.
[b]*T* scores ≤ 40 are in the clinical range.
[c]*T* scores ≥ 60 are in the clinical range.

score was from the referred sample *increased* fairly steadily with the magnitude of the scores. Users can refer to Table 6-3 to estimate the likelihood that particular competence and problem scores represent deviance severe enough to warrant concern.

SUMMARY

This chapter presented several kinds of evidence for the validity of YSR scores. *Content validity* is supported by the ability of most YSR items to discriminate significantly between demographically matched referred and nonreferred youths (documented by analyses presented in Chapter 7). *Criterion-related validity* is supported by the ability of the YSR's quantitative scale scores to discriminate between referred and nonreferred youths after demographic effects were partialled out. Clinical cutpoints on the scale scores were also shown to discriminate significantly between demographically matched referred and nonreferred youths.

Several procedures were presented for discriminating between youths like those in our referred versus nonreferred samples. One of the most effective ways to optimize discrimination is by classifying youths as normal if their total competence and problems scores are both in the normal range and as deviant if both these scores are in the clinical range. Youths who are in the normal range on one score and in the clinical range on the other are then classified as borderline between the two groups that are more clearly classifiable. Findings from discriminant analyses indicated the individual items and scales that contribute the most discriminative power when compared with all other items or scales.

Chapter 7
Item Scores

Beside being the basis for the YSR profile scales, the YSR items provide scores for specific competencies and problems, as reported by the subjects themselves. To determine which items discriminated significantly between youths referred for mental health services and nonreferred youths, we performed analyses of covariance (ANCOVA) on the item scores obtained by the demographically matched samples described in Chapter 6. The ANCOVA design was 2 (referral status) x 2 (sex) x 4 (ages 11-12, 13-14, 15-16, 17-18). The number of subjects per cell ranged from 59 for 17-18-year-old girls to 179 for 13-14 year-old girls, with a mean of 132 youths per cell. The total N was 2,108 with equal numbers of demographically-matched referred and nonreferred youths. SES was covaried using the 9-step Hollingshead (1975) scores for parental occupation. Ethnicity was covaried by creating a dummy variable scored 1 for white versus 0 for nonwhite and a second dummy variable scored 1 for black versus 0 for nonblack. There were not enough subjects of any one other ethnic group to warrant creating an additional dummy variable for another ethnic group.

COMPETENCE ITEMS

As reported in Chapter 6, the competence scales were included in the regression analyses of scale scores, but they were also included in the ANCOVAs reported here to provide direct comparisons with findings for the item scores. The competence scales and items were scored as they are scored on the YSR profile. For example, on Item *I. Please list the sports you most like to take part in*, a *0* is scored if the youth indicates either no sport or one sport. A *1* is scored if the youth lists two sports, and a *2* is scored if the youth lists three sports. Similar scores are assigned to the items for nonsports hobbies, games and activities, number of organizations, and number of jobs and chores. Appendix A provides the scoring rules for all the competence items.

Table 7-1 displays the ANCOVA results in terms of the percent of variance accounted for by each effect that was significant at $p < .01$. According to Cohen's (1988) criteria for the magnitude of effects in ANCOVA, effects accounting for 1 to 5.9% of variance are considered small, effects accounting for 5.9 to 13.8% of variance are medium, and effects account­ing for >13.8% of variance are large. Because the effect of each independent variable and covariate was tested for each of the 13 competence items, 2 scales, and total competence score, we have indicated with superscript *f* the 2 out of 16 effects that were most likely to be significant by chance, because they had the smallest *F* values (Sakoda et al., 1954).

Referral Status Differences in Competence Scores

As indicated in Table 7-1, Item *II.A. Number of nonsports activities* was scored significantly higher for referred than nonreferred youths. In addition, *Item I.A. Number of sports* was also scored higher for referred than nonreferred youths, although this difference was not significant ($p = .14$). As discussed in Chapter 2, these two items have therefore been omitted from the 1991 YSR Activities scale and total competence scores.

Nonreferred youths obtained higher scores than referred youths on all the remaining competence items, the two scales, and total competence. All the differences were significant ($p < .01$) except those on Items I.B., II.B., and VI.B. The largest differences accounted for 9% of the variance in Item *VI.A. Behavior with others* and the Social scale score, and 8% of the

Table 7-1
Percent of Variance Accounted for by Significant ($p < .01$) Effects
of Referral Status and Demographic Variables in ANCOVAs of
YSR Competence Items and Scales

	Ref Stat[a]	Sex[b]	Age[c]	RxA[d]	Covariates[e] SES	White	Black
I.A. Number of sports	--	--	2^Y	--	--	--	--
B. Sports part/skill	--	2^M	1^Y	--	$<1^f$	--	--
II.A. Number of activ	2^R	--	2^Y	--	<1	--	--
B. Activ part/skill	--	--	--	--	<1	$<1^f$	--
III.A. Number of organ	3	$<1^{Ff}$	--	2	3	<1	$<1^{Nf}$
B. Partic in organ	3	--	--	1	2	<1	$<1^N$
IV.A. Number of jobs	3	--	2^Y	--	$<1^f$	--	--
B. Job performance	1^f	$<1^{Ff}$	--	--	--	--	$<1^B$
V.A. Number of friends	3	--	--	--	--	--	--
B. Contacts with fr	1^f	1^M	--	$<1^f$	--	--	--
VI.A. Gets along	9	--	--	$<1^f$	--	--	$<1^B$
B. Works/plays alone	--	--	$<1^{NLf}$	--	--	--	--
VII. Mean acad perf	8	--	--	--	2	--	--
Activities scale	2	--	1^{Yf}	--	<1	$<1^f$	$<1^{Bf}$
Social scale	9	--	--	2	1	1	$<1^N$
Total competence	8	--	--	2	2	1	$<1^N$

Note. Items are designated with summary labels for their content. Numbers in table indicate percent of variance accounted for by each effect that was significant at $p < .01$. Total $N = 2,108$.
[a]All significant differences reflect higher scores for nonreferred youths except Number of Activities.
[b]F = females scored higher; M = males scored higher.
[c]NL = nonlinear effect of age; Y = younger youths scored higher.
[d]RxA = referral status x age.
[e]All significant SES effects reflect higher scores for upper SES. All significant white-nonwhite effects reflect higher scores for whites. B = higher scores for blacks; N = higher scores for nonblacks.
[f]Not significant when corrected for number of analyses.

variance in Item *VII. Academic performance* and in the total
competence score.

   The tendency for referred youths to report more activities
than did nonreferred youths is consistent with findings in our
analyses of the pre-1991 YSR profile (Achenbach & Edelbrock,
1987). It is also consistent with Zimet and Farley's (1987)
finding of more favorable self-ratings for activities by disturbed
than normal children on Harter's (1982) Perceived Competence
Scale for Children. Our analyses for the 1991 CBCL profile
(Achenbach, 1991b) revealed identical mean scores for parents'
reports of the number of nonsports activities among referred
and nonreferred children. This suggests that the sheer number
of activities is not currently a good discriminator, although it
did show a significant difference in favor of nonreferred
children assessed in the 1970s (Achenbach & Edelbrock, 1981).
It is nevertheless clinically useful to know what sports and
nonsports activities youths report liking. The hand-scored and
computer-scored profiles provide space for displaying the
scores for these items separately from the competence scales.

   There were no significant sex x age or 3-way interactions.
The one referral status x sex interaction accounted for <1% of
the variance. It is omitted from Table 7-1, because it was less
than the two expected by chance for each type of analysis. As
Table 7-1 shows, there were six significant referral status x age
interactions, the largest of which accounted for 2% of the
variance. All of these interactions reflected a tendency for the
differences between referred and nonreferred youths to be
greater at older than younger ages. These relations can be seen
for each score in Figure 7-1, where the data points correspond
to the cells of the 2 x 2 x 4 ANCOVAs. (Similar figures for
the scale scores were presented in Chapter 6.)

Demographic Differences in Competence Scores

   Table 7-1 displays the significant main effects of sex and
age, plus the significant effects of the SES, white versus

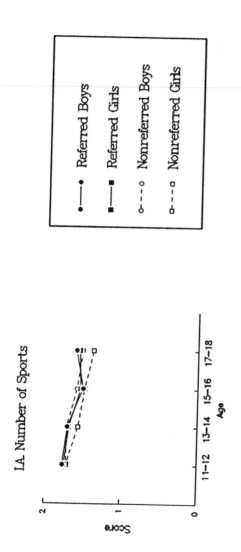

Figure 7-1. Competence items scored as they are on the YSR profile.

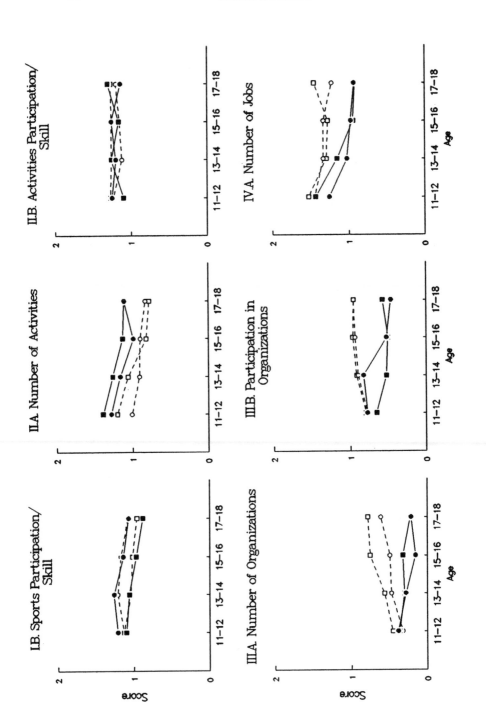

Figure 7.1 (cont.). Competence items scored as they are on the YSR profile.

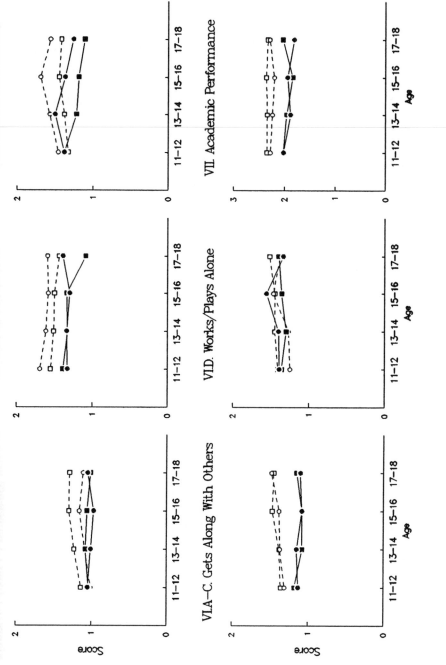

Figure 7-1 (cont.). Competence items scored as they are on the YSR profile.

nonwhite, and black versus nonblack covariates. Boys scored themselves higher than girls for Item I.B. and Item V.2., both small effects. Girls scored themselves higher than boys for Items III.A. and IV.B. Both of these effects accounted for <1% of the variance and could be considered chance findings, as they were the two smallest significant sex effects.

Younger youths scored themselves significantly higher on four items and the Activities scale, with the largest age effects accounting for 2% of the variance in Items I.A. and II.A., neither of which is counted in the 1991 competence scale scores, and in Item IV.A. There was also a nonlinear effect of age accounting for <1% of the variance in Item VI.A., which could be considered a chance finding.

All 10 SES effects reflected higher scores for upper SES youths, with the largest accounting for 3% of the variance in Item *III.A. Number of organizations.* The six effects of the white versus nonwhite covariate all indicated higher scores for whites, but the largest accounted for only 1% of the variance in the Social scale and total competence score. The black-nonblack covariate indicated higher scores for blacks on two items and the Activities scale, and for nonblacks on two items, the Social scale, and the total competence score. All these effects accounted for <1% of variance, except the 1% effect on the total competence score.

PROBLEM ITEM SCORES

The 0-1-2 scores on the problem items were analyzed for the 2,108 matched referred and nonreferred youths using the same 2 (referral status) x 2 (sex) x 4 (age level) ANCOVA design as was used for the competence items. SES, white versus nonwhite, and black versus nonblack were covariates, as they were in the ANCOVAs of competence items. Table 7-2 displays the ANCOVA results in terms of the percent of variance that was accounted for by each effect that was significant at $p < .01$. The 16 socially desirable items are also listed in the order of their sequence on the YSR. To take account of findings that might be significant by chance, we have indicated with superscript f the 5 out of 120 tests of each variable that were most likely to be significant by chance, because they had the smallest F values (Sakoda et al., 1954).

Referral Status Differences in Problem Scores

As Table 7-2 shows, referred youths scored significantly ($p < .01$) higher on all problem items except Items 2, 4, 7, 24, 29, 75, 83, and 93. Because Items 2. *Allergy* and 4. *Asthma* failed to discriminate significantly between referred and nonreferred samples on the CBCL as well as on the YSR, these items are omitted from the total problem score on the 1991 profiles, although their scores are displayed separately at the bottom of the YSR and CBCL profiles. (*Allergy* and *Asthma* do not appear on the TRF.) Item 7 was scored significantly higher for referred than nonreferred subjects at $p < .05$ on the YSR and $p < .01$ on the CBCL. The other five items all discriminated significantly between referred and nonreferred samples on the CBCL. To maintain comparability between the instruments, these items are retained for the total problem score on the YSR.

Differences between referred and nonreferred youths had a medium effect on the total problem score, accounting for 13% of the variance. Items *67. I run away from home* and *103. I am unhappy, sad, or depressed* showed the largest differences between referred and nonreferred youths, as indicated by the 10% of variance accounted for by referral status in both items. Item 67 is not on the TRF, but it showed a 5% effect of referral status on the CBCL. The smaller effect on the CBCL may reflect the inclusion of 4- to 10-year-olds, who run away less often than the 11- to 18-year-olds assessed with the YSR.

Table 7-2
Percent of Variance Accounted for by Significant (p <.01) Effects of Referral Status and Demographic Variables in ANCOVAs of YSR Problems and Socially Desirable Items

Item	Ref Stat[a]	Sex[b]	Age[c]	RxS	RxA	Covariates[e] SES	Black
1. Acts young	1	--	$<1^Y$	--	--	--	--
2. Allergy	--	--	--	--	--	$<1^U$	--
3. Argues a lot	3	--	--	--	--	--	--
4. Asthma	--	--	--	--	--	--	--
5. Acts like opposite sex	$<1^f$	2^F	--	--	--	--	--
6. Likes animals (SD)	--	--	$<1^Y$	--	--	--	<1
7. Brags	--	1^M	--	--	--	--	--
8. Can't concentrate	5	--	--	--	--	--	<1
9. Can't get mind off thoughts	3	--	$<1^O$	--	--	<1	--
10. Can't sit still	1	$<1^{Mf}$	--	--	--	--	--
11. Too dependent	1	--	--	--	--	--	--
12. Lonely	6	2^F	$<1^O$	--	--	--	--
13. Confused	7	2^F	$<1^O$	--	--	--	<1
14. Cries a lot	5	11^F	--	1	--	--	<1
15. Honest (SD)	4^N	$<1^F$	2^O	--	--	--	--
16. Mean to others	4	--	--	--	--	$<1^f$	--
17. Daydreams	2	$<1^F$	$<1^{NLf}$	--	--	--	$<1^f$
18. Harms self	6	2^F	--	1	--	--	--
19. Demands attention	1	--	--	--	--	--	--
20. Destroys own things	5	$<1^M$	--	--	--	--	--
21. Destroys others' things	3	--	--	--	--	--	--
22. Disobeys at home	5	--	--	--	--	--	<1
23. Disobeys at school	7	2^M	--	--	--	<1	--
24. Doesn't eat well	--	2^F	1^O	--	--	--	--
25. Doesn't get along	7	--	--	--	--	<1	--
26. Lacks guilt	1	--	--	--	--	--	--
27. Jealous	$<1^f$	1^F	$<1^O$	--	--	$<1^U$	<1
28. Willing to help (SD)	2^N	2^F	--	--	--	--	--
29. Fears	--	1^F	--	--	--	--	--
30. Fears school	3	$<1^{Ff}$	--	<1	--	--	--
31. Fears impulses	2	--	--	--	--	--	--
32. Needs to be perfect	<1	--	--	--	--	--	--
33. Feels unloved	7	2^F	--	<1	--	$<1^f$	$<1^f$
34. Feels persecuted	6	--	--	--	--	$<1^f$	<1

Table 7-2 (Continued)

Item	Ref Stat[a]	Sex[b]	Age[c]	RxS	RxA	Covariates[e]	
						SES	Black
35. Feels worthless	6	1[F]	--	<1[f]	--	--	<1
36. Accident-prone	1	--	1[Y]	--	--	--	--
37. Fighting	6	<1[M]	1[Y]	--	--	1	--
38. Is teased	1	--	3[Y]	--	--	--	--
39. Hangs around kids who get in trouble	4	1[M]	--	--	--	<1	<1[f]
40. Hears things	3	--	<1[NL]	--	--	<1[f]	--
41. Acts without thinking	3	--	--	--	--	--	<1[f]
42. Would rather be alone	2	<1[F]	<1[O]	--	--	--	--
43. Lying, cheating	4	--	--	<1[f]	--	--	--
44. Bites fingernails	<1	--	--	--	--	<1	--
45. Nervous	2	1[F]	<1[O]	--	--	--	<1
46. Nervous movements	2	--	--	--	<1[f]	--	--
47. Nightmares	2	2[F]	<1[NL]	--	--	--	--
48. Not liked	5	--	<1[Y]	--	--	<1	--
49. Can do things better (SD)	--	1[M]	--	--	--	<1	<1
50. Fearful, anxious	2	--	--	--	--	--	<1
51. Dizzy	4	<1[F]	--	--	--	--	--
52. Feels too guilty	4	<1[F]	--	--	--	--	--
53. Eats too much	<1	<1[F]	--	<1	--	--	--
54. Overtired	2	<1[F]	<1[O]	--	--	--	--
55. Overweight	1	4[F]	--	<1	--	--	--
56a. Aches, pains	2	<1[F]	--	--	--	--	--
56b. Headaches	2	2[F]	<1[Y]	<1[f]	--	--	--
56c. Nausea, feels sick	4	1[F]	<1[Y]	--	--	--	--
56d. Eye problems	2	--	--	--	--	<1	--
56e. Skin problems	1	<1[Ff]	--	--	--	--	--
56f. Stomachaches	3	4[F]	<1[NLf]	--	--	--	--
56g. Vomiting	2	--	1[Y]	--	--	--	--
56h. Other physical problems	<1	--	--	--	<1[f]	--	--
57. Attacks people	4	<1[M]	--	--	--	<1	--
58. Picking	<1[f]	--	--	--	--	--	--
59. Friendly (SD)	2[N]	<1[Ff]	--	--	--	--	--
60. Likes new things (SD)	<1[N]	--	--	--	--	--	--
61. Poor school work	6	<1[M]	--	--	--	--	<1
62. Clumsy	2	<1[F]	--	--	--	--	<1
63. Prefers older kids	2	<1[F]	3[O]	--	--	--	--

Table 7-2 (Continued)

Item	Ref Stat[a]	Sex[b]	Age[c]	RxS	RxA	Covariates[e] SES	Black
64. Prefers younger kids	1	--	--	--	--	--	--
65. Refuses to talk	5	--	--	--	--	--	$<1^B$
66. Repeats actions	2	--	--	--	--	--	--
67. Runs away from home	10	$<1^F$	$<1^O$	<1	$<1^f$	--	--
68. Screams a lot	4	4^F	--	<1	--	--	<1
69. Secretive	4	1^F	$<1^{Of}$	--	--	--	--
70. Sees things	5	--	--	--	--	<1	--
71. Self-conscious	$<1^f$	3^F	$<1^O$	--	--	--	<1
72. Sets fires	2	2^M	--	<1	--	--	--
73. Works well with hands (SD)	--	1^M	$<1^{NL}$	--	--	<1	--
74. Shows off	$<1^f$	2^M	--	--	--	--	--
75. Shy	--	2^F	$<1^O$	--	--	--	<1
76. Sleeps little	1	--	--	--	$<1^f$	--	$<1^f$
77. Sleeps much	1	--	$<1^O$	--	--	--	--
78. Good imagination (SD)	--	--	--	--	--	$<1^U$	--
79. Speech problem	1	--	$<1^{Yf}$	--	--	--	--
80. Stands up for rights (SD)	$<1^N$	--	$<1^O$	--	--	--	--
81. Steals at home	5	--	--	--	--	--	<1
82. Steals outside home	5	$<1^M$	--	--	--	--	--
83. Stores up unneeded things	--	--	--	--	--	--	--
84. Strange behavior	2	--	--	--	--	--	--
85. Strange thoughts	4	--	--	--	--	--	--
86. Stubborn	1	1^F	2^O	--	--	--	--
87. Moody	3	2^F	1^O	--	--	--	--
88. Enjoys others (SD)	3^N	$<1^F$	--	--	--	--	--
89. Suspicious	2	--	--	--	--	--	--
90. Swearing	5	$<1^{Mf}$	4°	--	--	--	<1
91. Suicidal thoughts	8	1^F	$<1^O$	1	--	--	--
92. Likes to make others laugh (SD)	3^N	--	--	--	--	--	--
93. Talks too much	--	4^F	--	--	--	--	<1
94. Teases a lot	<1	$<1^M$	--	--	--	--	--
95. Hot temper	5	--	$<1^O$	--	--	$<1^f$	--
96. Thinks about sex	3	2^M	3°	--	--	--	--
97. Threatens people	7	$<1^M$	--	--	--	<1	--

Table 7-2 (Continued)

Item	Ref Stat[a]	Sex[b]	Age[c]	RxS	RxA	Covariates[e] SES	Black
98. Likes to help (SD)	2^N	2^F	$<1^O$	--	--	--	--
99. Concerned with neat, clean	<1	$<1^F$	--	--	$<1^f$	<1	--
100. Trouble sleeping	5	1^F	--	$<1^f$	--	--	--
101. Truancy	7	--	5°	$<1^f$	--	--	--
102. Lacks energy	3	$<1^F$	--	--	--	--	--
103. Unhappy, sad, depressed	10	3^F	$<1^O$	<1	--	--	--
104. Loud	1	--	$<1^{Yf}$	--	--	--	--
105. Alcohol, drugs	6	--	7°	--	1	--	--
106. Fair to others (SD)	3^N	$<1^F$	$<1^O$	--	--	--	--
107. Enjoys jokes (SD)	3^N	--	--	--	--	--	--
108. Takes life easy (SD)	$<1^N$	--	--	--	--	--	--
109. Tries to help (SD)	3^N	2^F	$<1^O$	--	--	--	--
110. Wishes to be opposite sex	<1	3^F	--	--	--	--	--
111. Keeps from getting involved	3	--	--	--	--	--	--
112. Worries	3	3^F	$<1^O$	--	--	--	<1
Total Problems	13	1^F	--	<1	--	<1	<1

Note. Items are designated with summary labels for their content. SD indicates socially desirable items excluded from problem scale scores. Numbers in table indicate percent of variance accounted for by each effect that was significant at $p < .01$. Total $N = 2,108$.

[a]Nonreferred youths scored significantly lower on all problem items at $p < .01$ except Item 7, which was $p < .05$, and Items 2, 4, 24, 29, 75, 83, and 93, which were not significantly associated with referral status on the YSR. Nonreferred youths scored higher on all socially desirable items showing significant effects of referral status, as indicated by superscript N.

[b]F = females scored higher; M = males scored higher.

[c]NL = nonlinear effect of age; Y = younger youths scored higher; O = older youths scored higher.

[d]RxS = referral status x sex; RxA = referral status x age.

[e]All items showing significant SES effects were scored higher by lower SES, except those marked with superscript U. All items showing significant effects of the black-nonblack covariate were scored higher by nonblacks, except the ones marked with superscript B.

[f]Not significant when corrected for number of analyses.

Item 103 showed the largest difference between referred and nonreferred children on the CBCL/4-18 and one of the largest on the TRF (Achenbach, 1991b, 1991c).

Although many other items are also important in their own right and in their contributions to scale scores, the strong association of referral status with YSR, CBCL, and TRF scores for Item 103 indicate that self-, parent-, and teacher-reports of depressed affect should receive high priority in judging whether a youth is likely to need special help and in the evaluation of outcomes. This does not necessarily mean that all youths for whom Item 103 is reported should be diagnosed as having depressive disorders. On the contrary, depressive affect may be reported for many different reasons. Some youths who report depressive affect may not be deviant with respect to other aspects of a depressive pattern, such as those encompassed by the YSR Anxious/Depressed syndrome. Some youths who *are* deviant with respect to the syndrome, on the other hand, may also be deviant in other areas, indicating that their problems should not be interpreted in terms of depression alone. Still other youths may manifest depressed affect only in certain contexts. It is therefore important to consider reports of depressed affect in relation to multiple sources of data on multiple aspects of youths' functioning, rather than simply equating it with a depressive disorder.

As Table 7-2 shows, there was a small tendency (3% of variance) for girls to score higher than boys on Item 103. There were also very small tendencies for older youths to score higher and for the effects of referral status to interact with sex (both effects accounted for <1% of variance). The interaction reflected a tendency for girls' scores to be more elevated above boys' scores in the referred than nonreferred sample.

The following items also showed medium differences (≥5.9% of variance) between referred and nonreferred children: *13. I feel confused or in a fog* (7% of variance); *18. I deliberately try to hurt or kill myself* (6%); *23. I disobey at school* (7%); *25. I don't get along with other kids* (7%); *33. I feel that no one loves me* (7%); *34. I feel that others are out to get me* (6%); *35. I feel worthless or inferior* (6%); *37. I get in many fights* (6%); *61. My school work is poor* (6%); *91. I think about killing myself* (8%); *97. I threaten to hurt people* (7%); *101. I cut classes or skip school* (7%); and *105. I use alcohol or drugs for nonmedical purposes* (6%). As Table 7-2 shows, all demographic effects associated with these items were far smaller than the percent of variance accounted for by referral status, except for Item 101, where the tendency for older youths to score higher accounted for 7% of the variance, in addition to the 6% accounted for by referral status. Of the significant (p <.01) effects of referral status on the other items, 68 were small and 12 accounted for <1% of variance.

To provide a detailed picture of the prevalence rate for each problem item, Figure 7-2 displays the percent of youths who reported each problem (i.e., scored it 1 or 2). The data points correspond to the cells of the ANCOVAs, with youths grouped according to referral status, sex, and age.

Demographic Differences in Problem Scores

Table 7-2 displays significant main effects of sex and age, interactions of these variables with referral status, and effects of the SES and black-nonblack covariates. The white-nonwhite covariate, sex x age, and 3-way interactions are not displayed, because the few that were significant all accounted for <1% of variance. Only three effects of the sex x age and 3-way interactions reached p <.01, which is fewer than the five expected by chance (Sakoda et al., 1954). The white-nonwhite covariate showed higher scores for white youths on two items and higher scores for nonwhite youths on four items, all accounting for <1% of variance. This is only one more than the five significant effects expected by chance. In the 20 analyses showing significant SES differences, lower SES youths scored themselves higher for 17 items and total problems. Nine of the items and the total score showed the same tendency

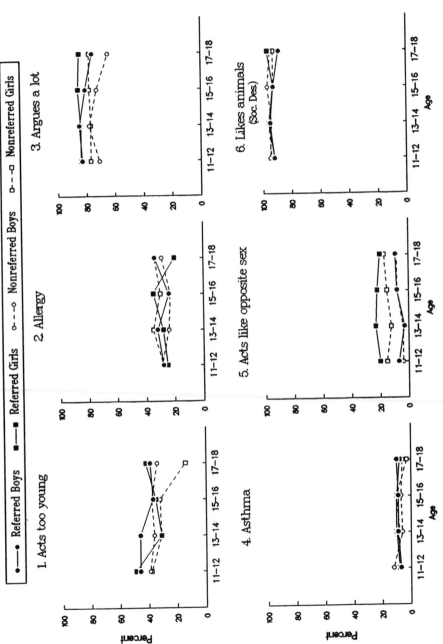

Figure 7-2. Percent of youths who reported each problem and socially desirable item.

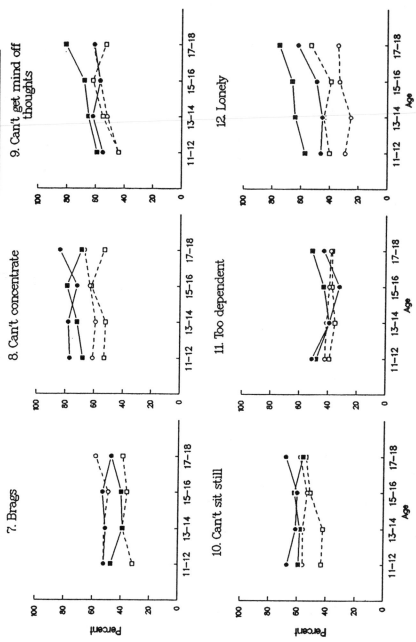

Figure 7-2 (cont.). Percent of youths who reported each problem and socially desirable item.

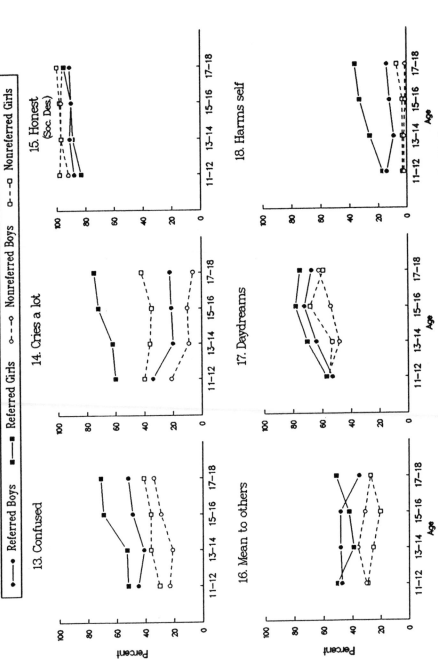

Figure 7-2 (cont.). Percent of youths who reported each problem and socially desirable item.

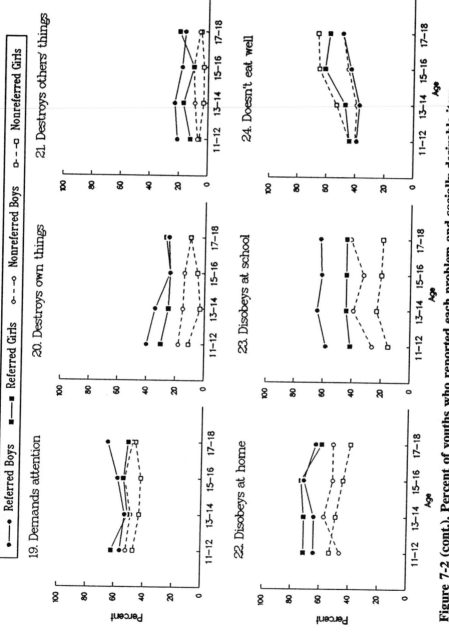

Figure 7-2 (cont.). Percent of youths who reported each problem and socially desirable item.

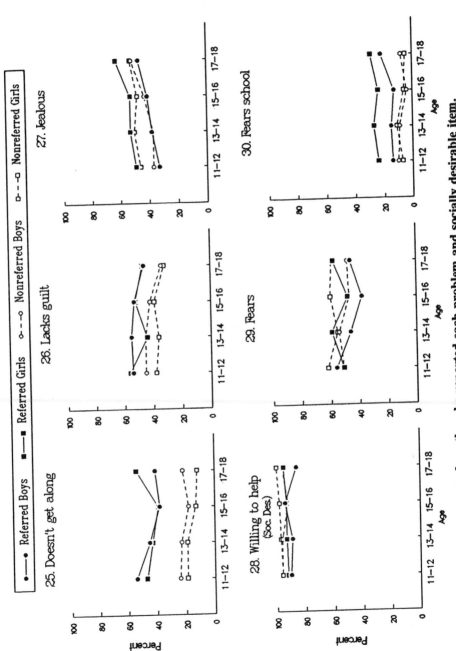

Figure 7-2 (cont.). Percent of youths who reported each problem and socially desirable item.

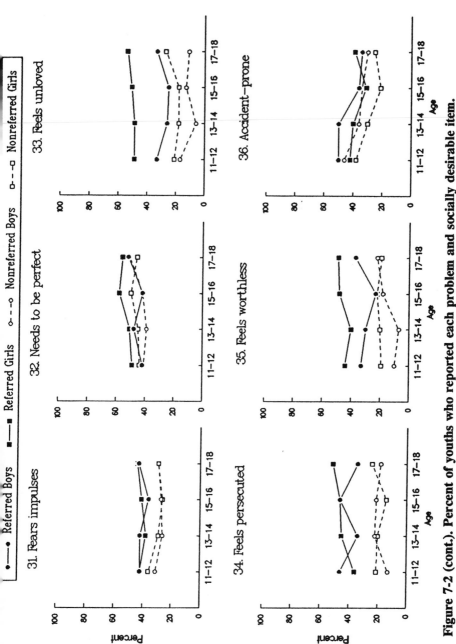

Figure 7-2 (cont.). Percent of youths who reported each problem and socially desirable item.

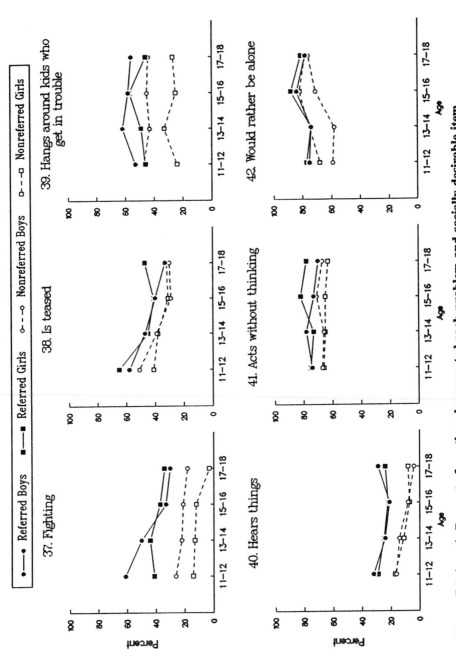

Figure 7-2 (cont.). Percent of youths who reported each problem and socially desirable item.

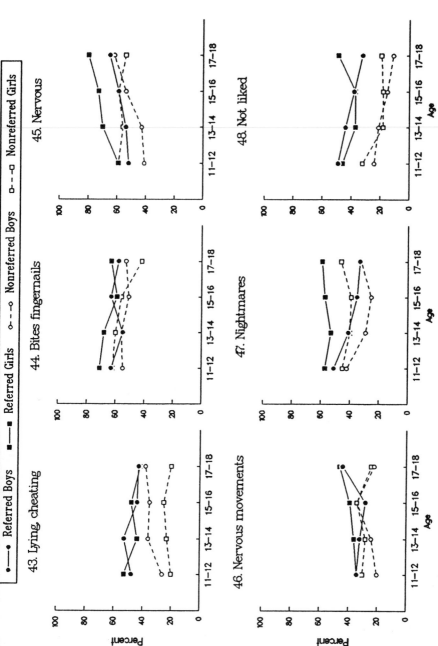

Figure 7-2 (cont.). Percent of youths who reported each problem and socially desirable item.

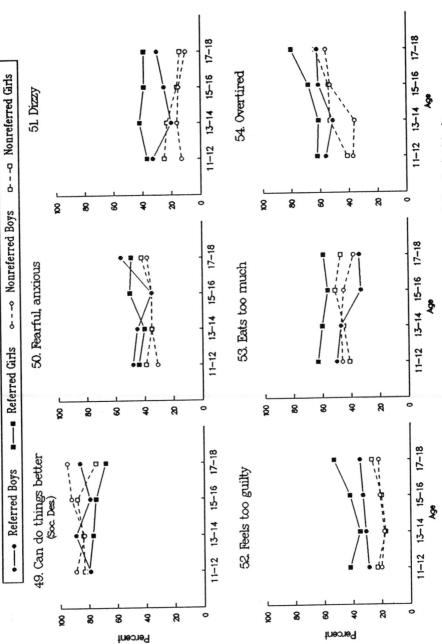

Figure 7-2 (cont.). Percent of youths who reported each problem and socially desirable item.

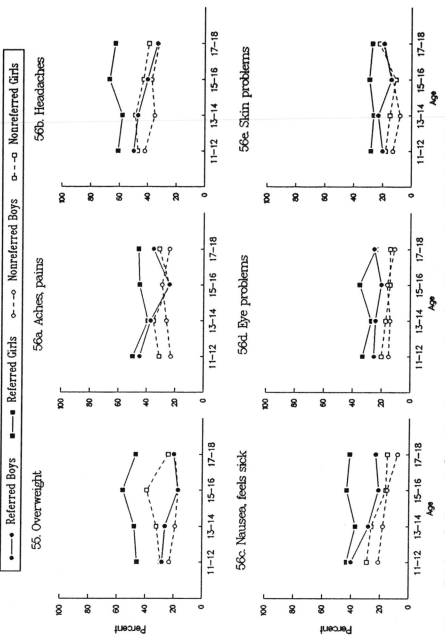

Figure 7-2 (cont.). Percent of youths who reported each problem and socially desirable item.

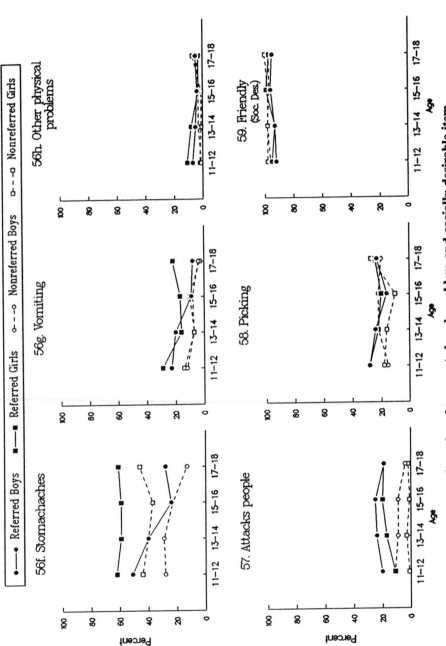

Figure 7-2 (cont.). Percent of youths who reported each problem and socially desirable item.

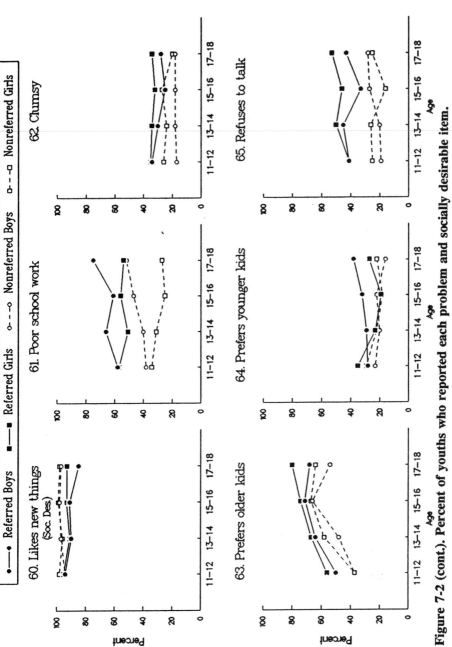

Figure 7-2 (cont.). Percent of youths who reported each problem and socially desirable item.

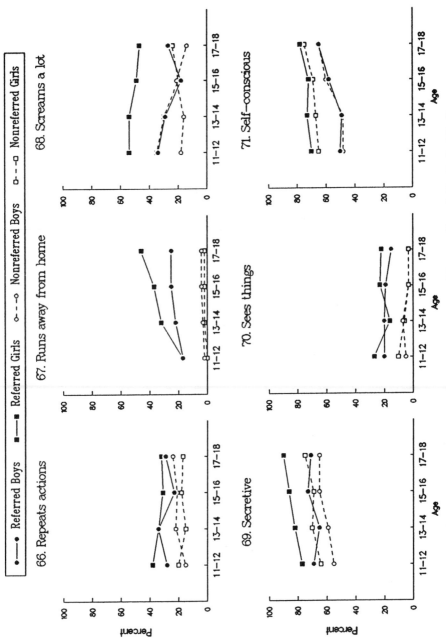

Figure 7-2 (cont). Percent of youths who reported each problem and socially desirable item.

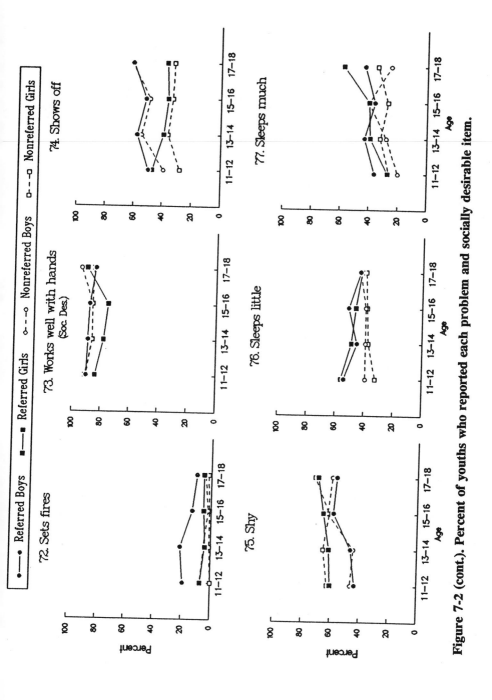

Figure 7-2 (cont.). Percent of youths who reported each problem and socially desirable item.

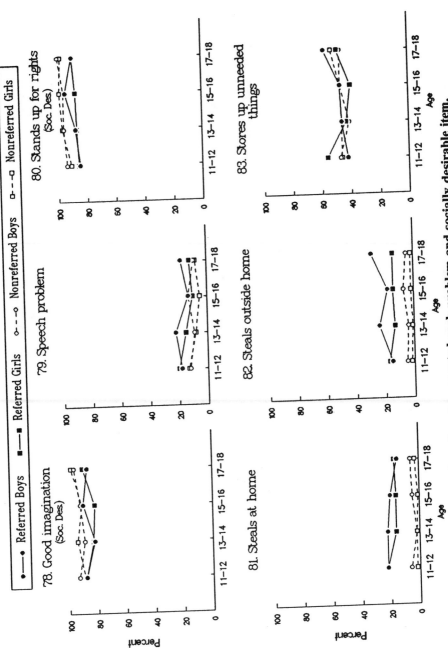

Figure 7-2 (cont.). Percent of youths who reported each problem and socially desirable item.

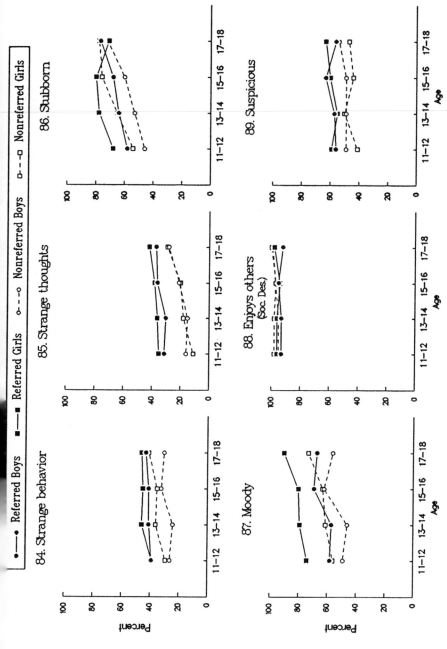

Figure 7-2 (cont). Percent of youths who reported each problem and socially desirable item.

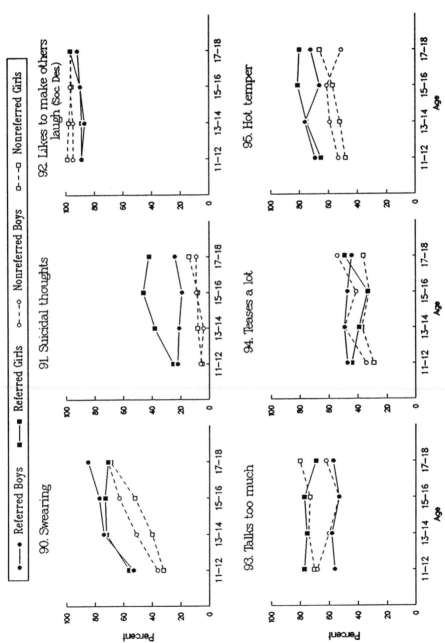

Figure 7-2 (cont.). Percent of youths who reported each problem and socially desirable item.

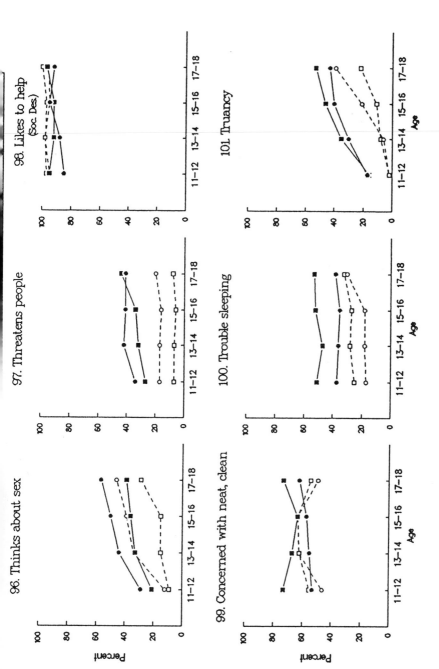

Figure 7-2 (cont.). Percent of youths who reported each problem and socially desirable item.

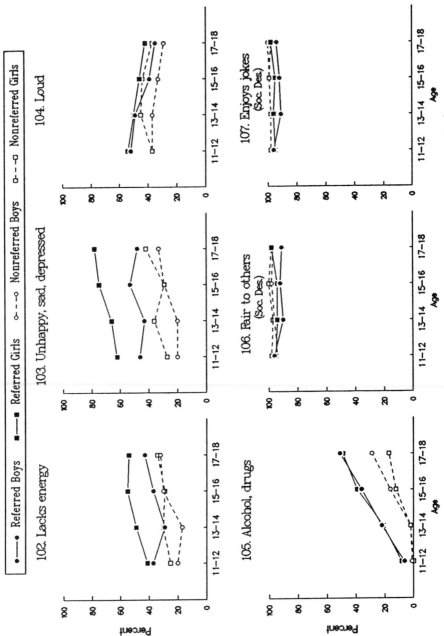

Figure 7-2 (cont.). Percent of youths who reported each problem and socially desirable item.

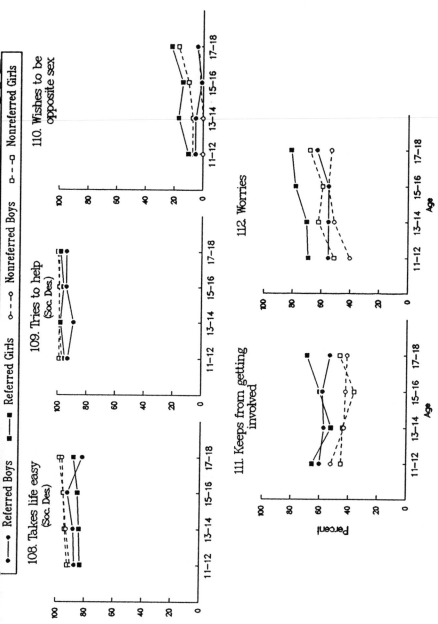

Figure 7-2 (cont). Percent of youths who reported each problem and socially desirable item.

for lower SES youths to report more problems in our previous YSR analyses, indicating stability in these small SES differences in YSR problem items (Achenbach & Edelbrock, 1987). As Table 7-2 shows, nonblacks scored themselves higher than blacks on 23 problem items and the total problem score, whereas blacks scored themselves higher on one problem item.

There were significant sex effects on 57 problem items, 42 of which were scored higher by girls and 15 by boys. Girls also obtained a significantly higher total problem score than boys, accounting for 1% of the variance. The largest sex difference accounted for 11% of variance in Item *14. I cry a lot*, where girls scored themselves higher. The item showing the largest effect of higher scores for boys was *74. I show off or clown*, where the sex difference accounted for 2% of the variance. Of the 22 Internalizing items that showed significant sex differences, all were scored higher by girls. Of the 19 Externalizing items that showed significant sex differences, 12 were scored higher by boys ($\chi^2 = 19.64, p < .001$). This highly significant tendency for girls to report more Internalizing problems and boys to report more Externalizing problems was consistent with parent- and teacher-reports across numerous cultures (Achenbach, Bird, Canino, Phares, Gould, & Rubio-Stipec, 1990; Achenbach, Hensley, Phares, & Grayson, 1989).

Linear age effects reflected significantly higher scores for older youths on 24 problems and for younger youths on 10 problems. An additional 4 problems showed nonlinear age effects, as indicated by the superscript *NL* in Table 7-2. The shapes of the age effects can be seen from the graphs of the item scores in Figure 7-2. The largest age effect accounted for 7% of variance in Item *105. I use alcohol or drugs for non-medical purposes*, where older youths scored themselves higher. No other age differences exceeded Cohen's criteria for small effects. Of the 13 Internalizing items showing significant age effects, 10 were scored higher by older youths. Of the 11 Externalizing items showing significant age effects, 9 were scored higher by older youths, a nonsignificant difference.

Three of the 16 significant interactions between referral status and sex accounted for as much as 1% of variance. These all reflected the tendency for girls to score themselves higher than boys to be especially pronounced among referred girls on Items *14. I cry a lot, 18. I deliberately try to hurt or kill myself,* and *91. I think about killing myself.*

Socially Desirable Items

As shown in Figure 7-2, all of the socially desirable items were endorsed by most youths. However, as can be seen from Table 7-2, nonreferred youths scored themselves significantly higher on Items 15, 28, 59, 60, 80, 88, 92, 98, 106, 107, and 108. Nonreferred youth also scored themselves higher on the remaining five socially desirable items, for which the associations with referral status were not significant.

To determine whether the socially desirable items would add to the discriminative power of the total competence score, we performed a 2 (referral status) x 2 (sex) ANCOVA on the sum of the socially desirable items and the competence score. This composite variable showed slightly *less* discrimination between referred and nonreferred youths than the total competence score alone.

Girls scored themselves significantly higher on socially desirable Items 15, 28, 59, 88, 98, 106, and 109, while boys scored themselves significantly higher on Items 49 and 73. The largest sex difference was on the similar items *28. I am willing to help others when they need help* and *109. I try to help other people when I can,* where the tendency for girls to score themselves higher accounted for 2% of variance.

Older youths scored themselves significantly higher on Items 15, 80, 98, 106, and 109, while younger youths scored themselves higher on Item 6, and there was a nonlinear age trend on Item 73. The largest age effect was on Item *15. I am pretty honest,* where the tendency of older youths to score themselves higher accounted for 2% of variance.

There were no significant interaction effects on the socially desirable items. Upper SES youths scored themselves slightly higher on Items 49 and 78, while they scored themselves lower on Item 73, all accounting for <1% of variance. The white-nonwhite covariate showed no significant effects, but nonblacks scored themselves higher on Item 6, while blacks scored themselves higher on Item 49, both accounting for <1% of variance.

SUMMARY

This chapter reported ANCOVAs of scores obtained by matched referred and nonreferred youths on the YSR competence items and scales, problem items, socially desirable items, and total problem score. Referred youths scored lower than nonreferred youths on all the competence items and scales, except for number of sports and nonsports activities, which are omitted from the 1991 Activities and total competence scales. Demographic differences in competence items were quite small. As on the CBCL and TRF, upper SES youths tended to obtain higher scores than lower SES youths, but these effects were smaller than the effects of referral status in most comparisons.

Referred youths scored themselves significantly higher on 95 of the 103 problem items. Because Items 2. *Allergy* and 4. *Asthma* did not discriminate significantly between referred and nonreferred samples on either the YSR or CBCL, they are not counted in the 1991 total problem score for either instrument. The other six YSR problem items that did not discriminate significantly at $p < .01$ were all scored higher by referred than nonreferred youths and did discriminate significantly at $p < .01$ on the CBCL. They have therefore been retained for the 1991 total problem score on both instruments.

Differences between referred and nonreferred youths accounted for 13% of the variance in the total problem score. The tendency for girls to report more problems accounted for

1% of the variance, but age had no significant effect on the total problem score. Lower SES youths and nonblack youths tended to report more problems than upper SES and black youths, but these effects accounted for <1% of the variance in the total problem score. Items *67. I run away from home* and *103. I am unhappy, sad, or depressed* showed the largest differences between referred and nonreferred youths, with referral status accounting for 10% of the variance in both items.

Most referred and nonreferred youths endorsed the socially desirable items. However, nonreferred youths obtained higher scores than referred youths on all of them, with most of the differences being significant.

Chapter 8
Relations Between Pre-1991
and 1991 YSR Scales

This chapter summarizes differences between the pre-1991 and 1991 YSR scales, the scales having counterparts in the two editions, and correlations between the counterpart scales.

Beside the differences in the scales themselves, an innovation applied to all the 1991 scales is the designation of a borderline range above the clinical cutpoint. The purpose is to emphasize that all scores are subject to variation and that a clinical cutpoint does not mark a definitive boundary between the normal and abnormal. For purposes of statistical analysis, a specific cutpoint is designated for each scale, but clinical evaluations of youths whose scores are within 3 T scores above the cutpoint should emphasize that they are in the borderline range.

Additional innovations include the following:

1. Normalized T scores were based on the midpoints between percentiles of the raw score distributions.

2. All syndrome scales were truncated at $T = 50$, rather than 55 as on the pre-1991 scales.

3. Gaps of more than 5 points between $T = 50$ and the next higher T score were limited by using the mean of $T = 50$ and the third highest T score.

4. $T = 89$ was assigned to the mean of the five highest raw scores obtained by our clinical samples on the Internal-

izing, Externalizing, and total problem scores, rather than being assigned to the highest scores, as was done to establish $T = 89$ on the pre-1991 scales.

5. Item 2. *Allergy* and 4. *Asthma* are omitted from the total problem score.

6. Internalizing and Externalizing scores can be computed from scale scores on the hand-scored profile without having to enter each Internalizing and Externalizing item's score.

CONSTRUCTION OF SCALES

Syndrome Scales

The pre-1991 profiles were developed separately for each sex on the YSR. Furthermore, the YSR scales were developed separately from the CBCL and TRF scales. Although the pre-1991 YSR norms for boys and girls were drawn from a single general population sample and the competence scales were similar for both sexes, the syndrome scales differed somewhat between the sexes on the YSR and differed from the CBCL and TRF syndrome scales.

As the use of the instruments spread and research advanced, closer integration of syndrome scales across sex/age groups and sources of data became more important. For research that involves both sexes, it is helpful to be able to compare them on similar scales. And the limited agreement among informants argues strongly for coordinating multisource data around similar foci.

As outlined in Chapter 3, the 1991 YSR syndrome scales were constructed by deriving *core syndromes* of items that were common to both sexes. Furthermore, the core syndromes derived from the YSR, CBCL, and TRF were compared to identify items common to each core syndrome in at least two of the three instruments. The items that were common to a core syndrome in at least two of the three instruments were used to defined a *cross-informant syndrome construct*. The items defining the construct represent an hypothetical variable that may underlie the varying manifestations reportable by youths, parents, and teachers. By including on the syndrome scales the items that were specific to the core syndrome derived from a particular type of informant, we retained those aspects of a syndrome that may be evident only to that type of informant. We thus retained variations in problem behavior that may differentiate between manifestations of particular syndromes in different contexts while advancing coordination of multiple data sources and highlighting elements of disorders that may be consistent across contexts.

In addition to the cross-informant syndromes, we identified a syndrome in boys' YSR responses that was designated as *Self-Destructive/Identity Problems*, because the items having the highest loadings included *5. I act like the opposite sex, 18. I deliberately try to hurt or kill myself, 91. I think about killing myself*, and *110. I wish I were of the opposite sex*. A version of this syndrome was also identified in the boys' data for the pre-1991 YSR profile (Achenbach & Edelbrock, 1987).

The 12 items of the Self-Destructive/Identity Problems syndrome are listed in Appendix A and are marked with superscripts on the hand-scored and computer-scored versions of the YSR profile for boys. The 12 items are summed to provide a total raw score for which T score equivalents can be obtained from Appendix A. The computer-scoring program automatically computes the raw scale scores and T scores, which are displayed in the lower right-hand corner of the printout.

The Self-Destructive/Identity Problems items contribute to the total problem score, as do the other YSR problem items. However, because the syndrome did not have counterparts in girls' YSR ratings, nor in the CBCL or TRF, it is regarded as an optional scale. Statistical comparisons with the pre-1991 version of the syndrome are presented later in this chapter.

Syndrome Scale Names. The 1991 Somatic Complaints, Delinquent Behavior, Aggressive Behavior, and Self-Destructive/Identity Problems scales have names similar to scales on the pre-1991 profile. The 1991 Anxious/Depressed syndrome is the counterpart of the pre-1991 YSR, CBCL, and TRF Depressed syndrome. This syndrome includes items indicative of both anxiety and depression. Some youths who score high on this syndrome scale may primarily have anxiety problems that would qualify for a DSM anxiety disorder diagnosis. Other youths who score high on the scale may primarily have depressive problems that would qualify for a diagnosis of depression.

Although people may be able to discriminate between their own feelings of anxiety and depression, our analyses indicate that these kinds of problems are closely intertwined in self-reports by clinically referred adolescents. Parents' and teachers' reports of anxiety and depression also tended to form a single syndrome on the CBCL and TRF. Many other studies have similarly found close associations between problems of anxiety and depression in the young (e.g., Bernstein & Garfinkel, 1986; Cole, 1987; Saylor, Finch, Spirito, & Bennett, 1984; Strauss, Last, Hersen, & Kazdin, 1988; Treiber & Mabe, 1987).

Our pre-1991 analyses did not identify an equivalent of the Withdrawn syndrome in the YSR responses. As explained in Chapter 3, an independent syndrome of this sort was not identified in our 1991 analyses, either. However, because the Withdrawn syndrome met our criteria for cross-informant syndrome constructs by being among the core syndromes for at least two of the three instruments (CBCL and TRF), it is available for scoring on the YSR. As reported in Chapter 6, the cross-informant Withdrawn syndrome did discriminate significantly between YSR ratings by referred versus nonreferred youths. However, users may choose to ignore it if they wish.

The 1991 Social Problems syndrome is a counterpart of the pre-1991 YSR Unpopular syndrome. The Thought Problems syndrome is a counterpart of the pre-1991 YSR Thought Disorder syndrome. A clear counterpart of the 1991 Attention Problems syndrome was not found in the pre-1991 YSR analyses. Nevertheless, the 1991 analyses for both boys and girls identified a core syndrome similar enough to the CBCL and TRF versions to be included in the comparisons with the core syndromes derived from parent- and teacher-ratings.

Internalizing and Externalizing

Like the syndrome scales, the pre-1991 Internalizing and Externalizing groupings were constructed separately for each sex/age group on the YSR, CBCL, and TRF. Although there were general similarities among the various versions of the Internalizing and Externalizing groupings, the precise compositions differed because of variations in the syndromes on which they were based. Furthermore, a few items were scored on syndromes from both the Internalizing and Externalizing groupings.

For the 1991 profiles, uniform Internalizing and Externalizing groupings were established by averaging the loadings obtained for each of the eight syndromes in separate second-order factor analyses of each sex/age group scored on the YSR, CBCL, and TRF. The three syndromes having the highest loadings on the second-order Internalizing factor and the two syndromes having the highest mean loadings on the second-order Externalizing factor were used to define the Internalizing and Externalizing groupings across all sex/age groups on the YSR, CBCL, and TRF.

Like the cross-informant syndromes, the 1991 Internalizing and Externalizing groupings are quite uniform, although there are also some variations reflecting the items of certain syndromes that are specific to one instrument. Unlike the pre-1991 versions, no items are scored on both Internalizing and Externalizing groupings. Only one item (*103. Unhappy, sad, or depressed*) is scored on two syndromes (Withdrawn and Anxious/Depressed) within one grouping. However, this item is counted only once toward the Internalizing score.

Total Problem Score

The 1991 total problem score differs from the pre-1991 version only with respect to the omission of items *2. Allergy* and *4. Asthma*, which did not discriminate significantly between referred and nonreferred samples on either the YSR or the CBCL. Because these problems may nevertheless be important in clinical evaluations of individual youths, they are retained on the YSR and their scores are displayed separately beneath the YSR profile.

STATISTICAL RELATIONS BETWEEN PRE-1991 AND 1991 SCALES

Table 8-1 presents Pearson correlations between the *T* scores of the pre-1991 and 1991 counterpart scales, scored for our 1991 referred and nonreferred samples combined. The correlations were in the .80s and .90s, except for the 1991 Social Problems scale for boys, for whom it correlated .78 with the pre-1991 Unpopular scale. For the girls, the correlation between these scales was .92.

The high correlations in Table 8-1 indicate that individual youths would have very similar rank orders in the distributions of scores on the pre-1991 and 1991 scales. Correlational analyses and other analyses of the relative magnitude of scores within particular distributions would thus produce similar results using the corresponding pre-1991 and 1991 scales. Because the precise content and number of items differed,

Table 8-1
Pearson Correlations Between Raw Scores
for 1991 and Pre-1991 Counterpart Scales of the YSR

Scale	Boys	Girls
N =	1,072	1,036
Competence[a]		
Activities	.84	.83
Total Competence	.94	.95
Problems		
Somatic Complaints	.90	.90
Anxious/Depressed[b]	.89	.96
Social Problems[c]	.78	.92
Thought Problems	.92	.89
Delinquent Behavior	.91	.89
Aggressive Behavior	.96	.92
Self Dest/Ident Probs	.93	---
Internalizing	.92	.97
Externalizing	.99	.97
Total Problems	1.00	1.00

Note. Subjects were matched referred and nonreferred samples combined. All rs were significant at p <.00001. Pre-1991 scales were the closest counterparts of the 1991 scales.
[a]Social scale is not shown because the pre-1991 and 1991 versions are identical.
[b]Pre-1991 scale was designated as Depressed.
[c]Pre-1991 scale was designated as Unpopular.

however, a particular scale score on a pre-1991 scale is not equivalent to the same score on the 1991 counterpart of the scale. In fact, t tests showed that the mean scores differed significantly between most of the pre-1991 and 1991 versions.

SUMMARY

This chapter presented similarities and differences between the pre-1991 and 1991 YSR scales, plus correlations between the counterpart scales.

Innovations in the 1991 scales include: Derivation of cross-informant syndrome scales that are common to both sexes and different ages scored on the YSR, CBCL, and TRF; provision of a borderline clinical range on each scale; normalized T scores based on midpoint percentiles; syndrome scales truncated at $T = 50$; deletion of Items 2. *Allergy* and 4. *Asthma* from the total problem scores; easier hand scoring of Internalizing and Externalizing.

Correlations between most pre-1991 scales and their 1991 counterpart scales were in the .80s and .90s, indicating great similarity in the rank ordering of youths on the counterpart scales. The only correlation below .83 was for the Social Problems scale among boys, where the correlation was .78.

The mean scores obtained on most of the pre-1991 scales differed significantly from those obtained on the 1991 scales, owing to differences in the number and content of their items. A particular score on a pre-1991 scale is thus not necessarily equivalent to the same score on the 1991 counterpart of the scale. Nevertheless, the very high correlations between most pre-1991 scales and their 1991 counterparts indicate that correlational analyses and other analyses involving the relative magnitude of scores within particular distributions would produce similar results on the pre-1991 and 1991 scales.

Chapter 9
Practical Applications
of the YSR and Profile

This chapter addresses applications of the YSR to making *practical decisions* about *particular* cases, groups, programs, policies, etc. Practical applications can be contrasted with *research applications*, discussed in Chapter 10, which aim to establish *principles* that are *generalizable* and *testable*. Designed for both practical and research applications, the YSR is intended to utilize the fruits of research to improve practical assessment and to enrich research by linking it to practical assessment procedures.

The standardized self-reports obtained with the YSR provide a common language for practitioners and researchers who have contact with adolescents in diverse contexts. The YSR also serves as a key component of multiaxial assessment, for which practical applications are detailed in the *Integrative Guide for the 1991 CBCL/4-18, YSR, and TRF Profiles* (Achenbach, 1991a).

In presenting practical applications, we do not offer clinical "interpretations." Although such interpretations are often sought from assessment instruments, we believe that the meaning and utility of assessment data depend on the situation in which they are to be used. In evaluating youths, the skilled practitioner applies knowledge and procedures developed on other cases to obtain a clear picture of the individual case. Our standardized assessment procedures obtain descriptive data in a standardized fashion, aggregated into empirically based scales and normed on large representative samples. These procedures aid the practitioner in identifying specific features of the youth as seen from particular perspectives and as compared with normative samples of peers. The profiles show the areas in which the youth is in the normal, borderline, or clinical range. The procedures presented in the *Integrative Guide* (Achenbach, 1991a) enable the practitioner to systematically compare data from multiple sources. Hundreds of published studies have reported correlates of the profile scales (Achenbach & Brown, 1991).

Our standardized assessment procedures and their numerous correlates can bring a great deal of knowledge to bear on the individual case. However, we feel that it would be wrong to provide "canned" interpretations as if they could be mechanically applied to each individual case. Our procedures can greatly improve the assessment and documentation of young people's functioning. Yet, the unique features of each case limit the accuracy with which any procedure can extrapolate clinical interpretations of behavioral/emotional problems to specific cases. Canned interpretations should not be allowed to substitute for the detailed study of the individual case. It is the practitioner who must integrate standardized assessment data with unique information to attain a comprehensive understanding of the case. The essence of clinical creativity is to synthesize diverse procedures and data into an optimal solution for each case.

Responsible practice requires practitioners to test their judgment against various kinds of evidence. The profiles facilitate this process by enabling practitioners to compare informants' descriptions with what similar informants report about normative samples of peers, as well as with the practitioners' own impressions. The profiles also make it possible to compare descriptions obtained at different points in time, such as at intake into a service, after an intervention, and at follow-up. In the following sections, we provide illustrations and guidelines for using the YSR in conjunction with the typical procedures of various settings.

APPLICATIONS IN
MENTAL HEALTH CONTEXTS

The YSR can be used in virtually all mental health settings that serve 11- to 18-year-olds. These settings include private practices, outpatient clinics, acute care hospitals, group homes, and residential centers. The YSR can be most useful if it is routinely obtained at intake for all cases. Routine use of the YSR provides standardized documentation of presenting problems and competencies for purposes of case records, accumulating experience with the YSR in the particular setting, and providing a baseline from which to assess change.

Intake and Evaluation

Most referrals of youths are initiated by adults, such as parents and teachers. Intake information comes mainly from adults, usually parents or parent surrogates. The CBCL is designed to obtain parents' descriptions of their children in a standardized format. In many settings, the CBCL can be obtained uniformly as part of the referral or intake process for virtually every case. The CBCL can be repeated at later points during and after an intervention to evaluate change as reported by parents.

When youths are brought for mental health services, they can be asked to fill out the YSR to obtain their views for comparison with their parents' CBCL, to provide a baseline for comparison with subsequent assessments, and to encourage expression of the youths' own concerns. Whereas the CBCL is typically completed by parents before their first clinical interview, the timing of the YSR depends more on individual circumstances. For most youths —especially those toward the upper end of the 11- to 18-year age range—the YSR can be completed before or at the initial contact, just as the CBCL is completed by parents before or at the initial contact. For youths who resist referral and deny needing help, one or two introductory clinical interviews may be required before they are cooperative enough to complete the YSR. On the other hand, some resistant youths are more willing to complete the YSR than to express themselves in an interview. Not only do their YSR responses provide information not obtainable via interview, but completing the YSR often encourages them to talk about themselves. In most situations, the YSR can be introduced as follows:

"I (or we) would like you to fill out this form in order to obtain your views of your interests, feelings, and behavior."

If a youth cannot read or has other problems in filling out the YSR, it is helpful to give the youth a copy of the YSR while an interviewer reads each item and enters the response. However, the focus should be on helping the youth respond accurately to the YSR rather than on probing for underlying determinants.

The youth should be assured of confidentiality, including confidentiality from parents. The clinician or someone else familiar with the YSR should be available to answer any questions the youth has while completing it. Questions should be answered in an objective and factual manner to help the youth understand the literal meaning of items, rather than to probe the youth's thoughts. If the YSR is administered orally, it should be done out of earshot of others. The completed YSR and the scored profile should not be accessible to unauthorized persons.

Clinical Interviewing

After the YSR has been completed and scored, it can help to guide clinical interviewing. Youths may spontaneously wish to discuss their responses or begin talking about issues broached on the YSR, such as suicidal ideation, strange thoughts, sexual identity problems, or feelings of rejection. The interviewer may wish to ask for clarification of certain items that the youth reports, especially such items as *9. I can't get my mind off certain thoughts; 40. I hear sounds or voices that other people think aren't there; 66. I repeat certain actions over and over; 70. I see things that other people think aren't there; 84. I do things other people think are strange;* and *85. I have thoughts that other people would think are strange.* Comments written by youths in the spaces beside items and in the spaces provided on pages 2 and 4 often help to explain their responses and provide material to be explored in clinical interviews.

After obtaining clarification of the youth's responses, the interviewer can use the items of greatest concern and the profile scales showing the most deviance as foci for interviewing about the history and context of the problems. Problem scales found to be well below clinical cutpoints can provide a basis for reassurance that concerns in these areas are within the normal range. The competence portion of the profile can also be used to identify areas in which youths report competencies on a par with those of their agemates versus areas that might be targeted for improvement.

As clinical contacts progress, the youth can be asked to complete the YSR again in order to assess changes in self-reported feelings and behaviors. Repeat YSRs can be used as a continuing guide for clinical interviews, including discussion of how the youth feels about changes that are or are not occurring. At each administration of the YSR, it can also be compared with other types of data in order to coordinate findings from different perspectives.

Planning Interventions

The interventions to be considered in a particular case depend on many factors. Examples include the reasons for referral; who is concerned about the youth's functioning; the family and school situation; the type of mental health service to which the youth is referred; and the youth's view of his or her own problems.

The YSR can be especially helpful in identifying ways in which youths' views of themselves differ from or resemble others' views of them. If a youth receives scores in the clinical range on the CBCL and TRF but reports few problems on the YSR, for example, this suggests either a lack of awareness or a lack of candor regarding problems reported by others. Before choosing an intervention, it would be important to determine whether the youth is truly unaware of the problems, is aware of them but unwilling to take responsibility for them, or whether the other informants' reports are questionable.

If it becomes clear that the youth refuses to acknowledge problems that are substantiated by others, this would argue against interventions that presuppose spontaneous motivation to change oneself. If the youth and other informants agree in reporting Externalizing problems, this would indicate that the youth's awareness of the problems is consistent with that of the other informants and that the youth may recognize the need for change.

If few Internalizing problems are reported on the YSR, this suggests a lack of the personal discomfort usually needed to motivate talking therapies, but behavioral or milieu approaches may be feasible. Youths who obtain scores in the clinical range on the Internalizing scales, on the other hand, may be better candidates for therapies that capitalize on feelings of discomfort with oneself.

Beside aiding in the choice of a general therapeutic approach, the YSR can help in selecting specific targets for change. This can be done by discussing with the youth the specific problems reported on the YSR that cause the most distress. It can also be done at the level of syndrome scale scores by targeting treatment on the syndromal areas that show the greatest deviance, such as those indicated by the Anxious/Depressed, Somatic Complaints, Social Problems, Thought

Problems, Self-Destructive/Identity Problems, Delinquent Behavior, or Aggressive Behavior scales. Problem areas that are substantiated by other assessment procedures but are not acknowledged by the youth may be targeted for bringing to the youth's attention.

Reassessments During and After Intervention

After an intervention begins, the YSR can be readministered periodically to track changes as they are seen by the youth. It is important to track changes across all problem areas, rather than reassessing only those areas that were targeted for change. Even though a youth was initially most deviant on the Aggressive Behavior scale of the YSR, for example, it is possible that a reduction of overt aggression may be followed by failure to improve or worsening in other areas, such as indicated by the Anxious/Depressed scale. Reassessments should therefore be used to provide continuing guidance for helping the youth, rather than merely determining whether the targeted problems have improved.

The YSR, CBCL, and TRF can all be used for post-treatment assessments to determine outcomes. It is especially useful to plan reassessments at uniform intervals for all cases in a caseload. For example, if all youths are scheduled to complete the YSR at intake and again at 6-month intervals thereafter, it is possible to accumulate data on the typical course of changes in that caseload. This can reveal the proportion who show major improvements versus no change or worsening. It can also be used to determine whether there are particular problems, types of cases, or family situations, for example, that show exceptionally good versus poor outcomes with particular interventions.

If parents and teachers are available, the CBCL and TRF can be readministered at the same intervals to determine whether similar patterns of change are reported by the different informants. In some cases, favorable changes reported on the

YSR may not be borne out by the CBCL or TRF, or vice versa. Such findings would suggest a need for altering interventions to facilitate improvement in the areas that failed to improve.

Case Example

The precise point at which the YSR is obtained in an evaluation and the choice of additional assessment procedures depend on the nature of the setting and the particular case. Figure 9-1 schematically depicts a sequence applicable to diverse clinical settings. The specific procedures may vary from case to case, with some of the listed procedures being omitted or used in different order, while procedures not listed in Figure 9-1 are also used. A family therapist, for example, may prefer to conduct all interviews conjointly with parents and the youth, rather than separately. If a youth is not attending school, the TRF and DOF would not be used. Psychological tests would not be administered if adequate test data were already available.

The following case illustrates the integration of the YSR with other procedures according to the general sequence depicted in Figure 9-1. To highlight the overall assessment model, we have omitted many clinical details, discussion of etiological factors, and consideration of alternative procedures.

Referral and Intake Assessment. Ginny, a 16-year-old 10th grader, was brought to a mental health clinic by her parents after a brief hospitalization for an overdose of aspirin.

Ginny had previously threatened suicide, but this was her first attempt. She had left a suicide note where her mother found it after she had ingested about 25 aspirin. She was taken to a hospital where her stomach was pumped and she remained overnight for observation. Her attending physician referred her to the local mental health clinic, where her parents brought her the following day.

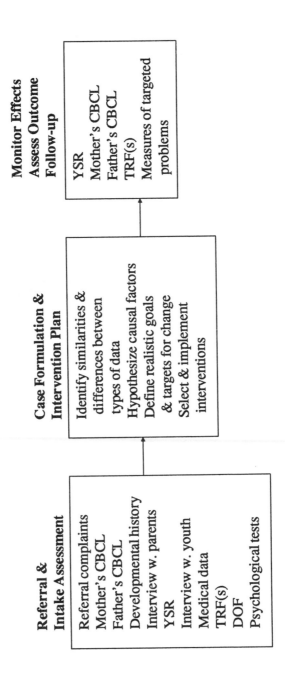

Figure 9-1. Schematic sequence for assessment of youths referred for mental health services. (Not all procedures would be used in all cases.)

As part of the clinic's routine intake procedure, both parents were asked to complete separate CBCLs, while Ginny was asked to fill out the YSR. They were assured of confidentiality and were asked to fill out the forms to reflect their own views, without consulting each other. While the CBCLs and YSR were being scored on a microcomputer, the parents completed the clinic's intake information form, which requested a developmental history and other background information. The completed CBCLs and YSRs and their scored profiles were given to the clinician who interviewed Ginny, followed by her parents, and then all three together.

Ginny's YSR yielded a total competence T score of 40, falling at approximately the 16th percentile for 11- to 18-year-old girls. Both her Activities and Social scale scores were at the low end of the normal range. On item V, regarding close friends, Ginny reported having only one friend and having less than one contact per week with any friends. Her mean Academic Performance score was 1.5, reflecting two ratings of below average and two ratings of average for her performance in academic subjects. In the space on page 2 for describing school concerns and problems, she wrote "I used to like school, but now I hate going there at all."

On the YSR problem items, Ginny's total T score was 74, which was well above the T score of 63 that marks the top of the YSR borderline range. As Figure 9-2 shows, her scores on the Somatic Complaints and Social Problems scales were above the borderline range, while her scores on the Withdrawn, Anxious/Depressed, and Attention Problems scales were in the borderline range. Her scores on the other syndrome scales were all within the normal range.

On the CBCL competence scales, both parents' ratings were in general agreement with Ginny's, indicating activities, social, and school functioning toward the low end of the normal range. On the CBCL syndrome scales, ratings by Ginny's mother were in the clinical range on the Withdrawn, Somatic Complaints, and Anxious/Depressed scales, but in the normal range on the

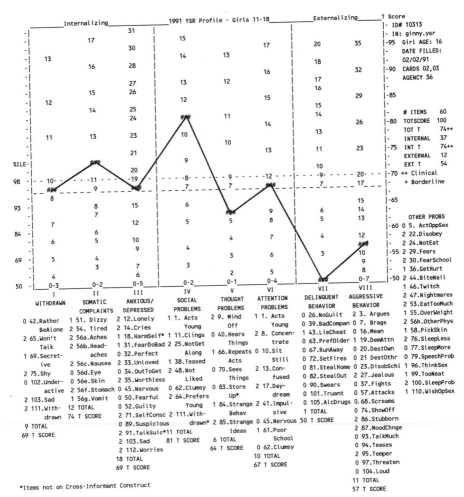

Figure 9-2. Computer-scored YSR problem profile for 16-year-old Ginny.

remaining five scales. Ratings by Ginny's father were in the clinical range only on the Anxious/Depressed scale. The total problem T scores of 73 on the mother's CBCL and 67 on the father's CBCL were both well above the T score of 63 that marks the top of the CBCL borderline range for 12-18-year-old girls.

Interviews with Ginny and her parents indicated that school was a major focus of her problems. Several months earlier, the family moved to an urban area where Ginny entered a much larger and more diverse high school than in the small town where they previously resided. She had previously obtained good grades with little effort and had neighborhood friends with whom she went to school. In the new school, by contrast, she found it harder to get good grades and had not made new friends. The one close friend she indicated on the YSR lived in the town where the family had previously resided.

Because school was such an important issue and because the Social Problems scale showed the greatest deviance on her YSR profile, Ginny and her parents were asked for permission to obtain TRFs from her teachers. They granted permission to obtain TRFs from Ginny's math and history teachers who, they felt, were the only ones who knew her well enough to be helpful. Neither teacher knew about Ginny's suicide attempt.

The TRF completed by Ginny's history teacher yielded academic performance, adaptive functioning, and total problem scores in the normal range. Only the Withdrawn scale was in the borderline range, with a T score of 69. The TRF completed by Ginny's math teacher showed academic performance and adaptive functioning at the low end of the normal range, but a total problem T score above the borderline range. The Withdrawn scale scored from the math teacher's TRF was in the borderline range. However, the Attention Problems scale scored from the math teacher's TRF was in the clinical range.

The comments written by the teachers on the TRF indicated that Ginny appeared to be an average though somewhat immature student in history, but was having problems in math that her teacher thought reflected inattention and lack of motivation. Neither teacher indicated any suicidal tendencies.

Test data from school records indicated that Ginny had obtained group IQ test scores ranging from 111 to 119 and achievement test scores in the average range. Because there was no reason to doubt these measures of her ability and achievement, cognitive testing was not done as part of the clinical evaluation. The medical work-up while she was in the hospital revealed no physical problems beside aftereffects of the aspirin overdose.

Formulation and Intervention. The low score on the YSR Thought Problems scale and the lack of any other evidence for poor reality testing or strange behavior on the CBCLs and TRFs indicated that psychotic tendencies were unlikely to be involved in Ginny's suicide attempt. Although her parents' CBCLs yielded scores in the clinical range on the Anxious/ Depressed scale, both scores were only moderately elevated. Ginny's score on the YSR Anxious/Depressed scale was in the borderline clinical range, but her score was much higher on the YSR Social Problems scale. Neither teacher reported enough problems on the TRF Anxious/Depressed scale to put it in the clinical range. Although Ginny was not a very happy girl, extreme depression did not appear to account for her suicide attempt.

A comparison of the profiles obtained from Ginny's YSR, her parents' CBCLs, and her teachers' TRFs indicated that her severest problems concerned feelings of rejection by peers, as manifest in her high score on the Social Problems scale of the YSR. Her teachers also reported some problems in peer relations, but not enough to be clinically deviant on the Social Problems scale. Instead, both her teachers reported problems in the borderline range on the Withdrawn scale, whereas her math teacher reported more problems on the Attention Problems scale. Her father's CBCL reflected mainly problems on the Anxious/Depressed scale that were evident in his presence, whereas her mother's CBCL reflected additional problems of somatic complaints and withdrawal that Ginny expressed to her.

Although most of Ginny's problems might be considered reactive to the family's move and her new school environment, the history obtained from her parents indicated that she had milder versions of similar problems where they had previously lived. Family tensions had also increased after the move, because of the demands of the father's new job. The TRF ratings suggested that Ginny was not actively rejected by peers, but that she reacted to new challenges—such as the math curriculum—with inattention, as well as withdrawal.

Although her family's move and new school were not the only causes of Ginny's problems, they were the main foci of her concerns. Because her social and educational development was being impeded, it was decided to capitalize on her distress about peer relations to motivate the acquisition of new skills needed to advance her social and academic development. Her therapist met with her for five weekly sessions in which risks of suicide were evaluated and a plan for participation in a social skills group lead by another therapist was explored.

Because the risk of suicide seemed minimal, the individual therapy sessions were reduced to once a month for the next four months while Ginny attended the social skills group. The group was composed of youths who were having social and academic problems related to anxiety, feelings of rejection, poor peer relations, and the pressures of large urban schools. Several group members had made suicide attempts and most had at least contemplated suicide. The emphasis was on understanding that peers have similar problems, that such problems can be brought into the open, and that there are ways of overcoming them.

Outcome Assessment. A month after the social skills group ended, Ginny's therapist asked her to complete the YSR again, while both parents completed CBCLs. Her math and history teachers, who did not know of her social skills group attendance, completed TRFs. The YSR profile showed a substantial drop in the Social Problems scale, which was now at the 93rd percentile of the normal range. The Anxious/ Depressed scale also dropped from the 97th percentile to the 84th, while the Somatic Complaints scale dropped from the clinical range to the 98th percentile cutpoint. The YSR total problem T score dropped from 74 to 59, which is just below the clinical cutpoint of 60. The CBCLs completed by both parents also showed decreases in total problem scores to the high normal range, as did the TRF completed by the math teacher. The scores on the TRF completed by the history teacher were all in the normal range.

Ginny had made some friends, accepted her new school situation, and seemed better able to cope actively with problems. She now denied contemplating suicide, but her therapist asked her and her parents to call if new problems arose. A follow-up six months later showed all CBCL and YSR problem scales in the normal range, although the YSR Somatic Complaints scale remained in the borderline clinical range, reflecting Ginny's longstanding tendency to react somatically to minor stress.

APPLICATIONS IN SCHOOL CONTEXTS

As illustrated in the preceding case, referrals of youths for mental health services often involve school-related problems and assessment data. The YSR can also be used for assessment and services within school systems.

Mandates for schools to provide special services—such as Public Law 94-142, the Education of All Handicapped Children Act—require systematic documentation of needs on which to base special services. As detailed elsewhere (Achenbach, 1991c; Achenbach & McConaughy, 1987), the TRF can provide a cornerstone for most school-based assessments. Even if pupils are learning disabled (LD), educable mentally retarded

(EMR), or physically handicapped, the TRF can document behavioral/emotional problems and adaptive characteristics that are important in planning and evaluating services for these pupils. If LD, EMR, and handicapped pupils have a mental age of at least 10 years, the YSR can document their own perceptions of their problems and competencies for use in planning and evaluating school-based services.

For pupils whose eligibility for special services is not so obvious, the YSR, TRF, CBCL, and DOF can contribute to the determination of eligibility. These instruments can play an especially crucial role in documenting eligibility for services to the severely emotionally disturbed (SED) and for determining whether pupils are more appropriately considered SED or LD. Table 9-1 outlines P.L.94-142 criteria for SED that can be assessed in terms of the YSR, TRF, CBCL, and DOF.

If referred pupils do not show deviance on any of the scales relevant to the SED criteria, they are unlikely to qualify for SED services under most interpretations of P.L.94-142. If they do show deviance on scales relevant to the SED criteria and also show evidence of a learning disability, then services should be planned to address both types of problems. It should be remembered that categories such as SED and LD are designed for administrative purposes to determine eligibility for special education services. The categories are not mutually exclusive, and most pupils do not fall neatly into only one category. Instead, pupils who have emotional problems often have learning problems and vice versa. Beside aiding in the administrative determination of eligibility for services, the YSR, TRF, CBCL, and DOF should therefore be used to tailor services to the pupil's specific needs, regardless of the administrative category of services. The following case illustrates the use of the YSR, TRF, CBCL, and DOF in school-based assessment to determine eligibility for services.

Table 9-1
Applications of the CBCL, YSR, TRF, and DOF to P.L. 94-142 Criteria for Serious Emotional Disturbance

P.L. 94-142 Components of SED	CBCL	YSR	TRF	DOF
Inability to learn	Attention Problems	Attention Problems	Attention Problems	On task
Inability to build or maintain relationships	Social Problems Withdrawn	Social Problems Withdrawn	Social Problems Withdrawn	Withdrawn-Inattentive
Inappropriate types of behavior or feelings	Aggressive Behavior Thought Problems	Aggressive Behavior Self-Destructive/Identity Problems[a] Thought Problems	Aggressive Behavior Thought Problems	Attention-Demanding Aggressive Behavior Hyperactive Nervous-Obsessive
General pervasive mood of unhappiness	Anxious/Depressed	Anxious/Depressed	Anxious/Depressed	Depressed
Tendency to develop physical symptoms or fears	Somatic Complaints	Somatic Complaints	Somatic Complaints	—

Schizophrenic	Thought Problems	Thought Problems	Thought Problems	—
Long period of time	Follow-up evaluations	Follow-up evaluations	Follow-up evaluations	Follow-up evaluations
Marked degree	Total, Internalizing, or Externalizing T score ≥ 60	Total, Internalizing, or Externalizing T score ≥ 60	Total, Internalizing, or Externalizing T score ≥ 60	Total score >93rd %ile
	Syndrome T score ≥ 67	Syndrome T score ≥ 67	Syndrome T score ≥ 67	Syndrome >98th %ile
Adversely affects educational performance	School scale T score ≤ 33	—	School performance T score ≤ 40 Adaptive functioning T score ≤ 40	—

[a]Scored for boys only.

Case Example

Referral. Allen, a 12-year-old seventh grader, was referred to the school psychologist by his English teacher after a temper outburst in which he started hitting two other boys in class. The outburst was evidently provoked by some subtle teasing, but the teacher had been concerned for several months about Allen's over-sensitivity to criticism, his inattention, and poor achievement.

Allen's cumulative record showed a longstanding pattern of marginal grades and achievement test scores in the low average range, somewhat below his IQ test scores, which were generally around 100. His record also contained occasional comments about inattention and immaturity, but no evidence of serious behavior problems.

Assessment. As part of the referral procedure, Allen's English teacher was asked to complete the TRF. When scored on the TRF profile, her ratings indicated academic performance and adaptive characteristics close to the bottom of the scales. The total TRF problem score of 80 was well above the borderline range for 12-18-year-old boys. The Attention Problems and Aggressive Behavior scales were both in the clinical range, while the Social Problems and Withdrawn scales were in the borderline clinical range. It was thus clear that the English teacher was reporting enough problems to warrant further evaluation and determination of eligibility for special services.

Allen's mother, who was a single parent, granted permission for a complete evaluation and agreed to fill out the CBCL. Allen's other teachers were asked to complete TRFs, and the school psychologist observed Allen and two comparison boys in three classes, using the DOF.

Scores on the TRFs ranged from the normal range for ratings by a science teacher who indicated that he did not know Allen well, to a total problem T score of 82 from a social studies teacher who reported more problems on the Social Problems and Withdrawn scales than the English teacher had.

The school psychologist observed Allen and two other boys for 10 minutes each in three classes. Allen showed more problems than the other boys during the observation sessions (mean score = 8.5 versus 1.0 for the mean of the two comparison boys), and was on task much less of the time (39% versus 93% for the mean of the two comparison boys). Allen's total DOF problem score was above the clinical cutpoint. The psychologist did not observe much aggressive behavior, but Allen's scores on the Withdrawn-Inattentive and Anxious/Depressed scales of the DOF were above the clinical cutpoint.

When interviewed by the school psychologist, Allen gave uninformative, monosyllabic replies to questions about his temper outburst. Owing to doubts about Allen's reading skills, the psychologist handed him a copy of the YSR and said he would read the items aloud. After the first few items, Allen began answering the questions without waiting for them to be read, indicating that his reading skills were adequate for the YSR. He was then allowed to complete the rest of the YSR on his own. The YSR profile showed that Allen acknowledged enough aggressive behavior like that reported by his English teacher to yield a score on the Aggressive Behavior scale in the clinical range. However, he also reported enough problems on the Anxious/Depressed and Social Problems scales to put both of them in the clinical range as well.

On the CBCL, Allen's mother reported few activities or social contacts and mediocre school functioning, resulting in a total competence score in the clinical range. On the problem portion of the CBCL profile, she reported enough problems of the Withdrawn, Social Problems, and Aggressive Behavior scales to put all of them in the clinical range. In an interview with the school psychologist, she indicated that Allen had always been somewhat shy and uncommunicative, but that, since his father had left the family a year ago, he had become moody, hostile, and angry.

Determination of Eligibility. In terms of the P.L.94-142 criteria listed in Table 9-1, Allen would not have been eligible for special services on the basis of learning disabilities or on the basis of the referral complaints of aggressive behavior, since his state's interpretation of P.L.94-142 did not include aggression as a basis for SED eligibility. However, his TRF, DOF, YSR, and CBCL total problem scores in the clinical range and his low school scale scores were evidence for emotional disturbance of a marked degree that adversely affected his educational performance. SED eligibility was supported by his own reports of problems sufficient to yield YSR Anxious/Depressed and Social Problems scores in the clinical range, corroborated by the psychologist's DOF ratings and scores in the clinical range for the Withdrawn scale on TRFs from two teachers and the CBCL from his mother. Taken together, these findings supported a determination that Allen met the P.L.94-142 criteria for "inability to build or maintain relationships" and "general pervasive mood of unhappiness."

Beside being used to determine eligibility, the data obtained with the YSR, TRF, CBCL, and DOF can be used to select specific targets for change through special educational services. The instruments can then be readministered to monitor change and to fulfill requirements for periodic re-evaluation of pupils receiving special educational services. If a youth's needs cannot be met within the school system, the data obtained with our instruments can be used to support referral for outside services, such as residential treatment.

Confidentiality in School Settings

Confidential data present special problems in schools. Most schools maintain a cumulative record on every pupil that includes grades, teachers' comments, and group test scores. Such records are usually available to teachers, but may often be accessible to others as well, even including pupils who help in school offices. Because pupils filling out the YSR should be assured of confidentiality, their responses and their YSR profiles should not be accessible to unauthorized people. The following safeguards of confidentiality should be observed:

1. Unless YSRs are to be completed anonymously for group studies or needs assessments, parental permission should be obtained for individual evaluations in which the YSR is employed.

2. The YSR should be administered to the pupil by a professional, such as a school psychologist, who is trained in assessment of youth psychopathology. The professional should tell the pupil the reason for the assessment, assure confidentiality, answer the pupil's questions, and administer the YSR orally if reading is a problem. Although pupils whose reading skills are adequate can fill out the YSR alone, the professional should remain available to answer questions.

3. Youths respond to the YSR not only with self-ratings, but also with comments that are personally revealing. It is therefore essential that the YSR be scored only by people who will protect its confidentiality and that the completed YSR and scored profile not be left in cumulative records or in other locations where its confidentiality may be compromised. Instead, it should be protected in the same way as other highly confidential material, such as psychological test reports.

APPLICATIONS IN MEDICAL CONTEXTS

Medical providers are often in a position to identify behavioral/emotional problems and to respond to the concerns that youths and their families may have. The YSR can be obtained routinely by physicians, health maintenance organizations, pediatric psychologists, and other providers by having youths complete it while waiting for their appointments. A receptionist can score the YSR by hand or microcomputer and give the completed YSR and scored profile to the provider. A glance at the profile can alert the provider to areas of deviance that need exploration with the youth. The profile can also be used as a basis for answering questions raised by a youth or parent about whether certain problems are normal for the youth's age.

Youths who have a serious physical illness or handicap may have concomitant behavioral or emotional problems. Such youths may be restricted from activities that are important in their peer group, may be teased or ostracized, may be impeded in school work, and may suffer discomfort or anxiety because of their condition.

The CBCL, TRF, and DOF can be used to pinpoint specific ways in which the problems and competencies of such youths differ from those of normative samples of agemates, as seen by other people. This can be helpful in planning placements and in identifying areas in which an ill or handicapped youth may need special help in adapting to peer groups. The YSR can likewise be helpful in identifying emotional problems that may not be apparent to others. Youths often report more internalizing problems on the YSR than are reported by adults on the CBCL, TRF, or DOF. The internalizing problems reported by ill and handicapped youths may be especially useful for identifying the subjective concerns with which the youths need help in adapting to their physical conditions.

For professionals who specialize in work with youths having a particular type of illness—such as diabetes or leukemia—or handicap—such as deafness or cerebral palsy—the YSR can be used to determine what concerns are most common among them and how these concerns differ from those of healthy youths. Once such concerns have been identified, therapy and support programs can be designed to focus on them. The efficacy of interventions can also be evaluated by readministering the YSR to assess reductions in these concerns.

FORENSIC APPLICATIONS

The YSR can be used in a variety of court-related evaluations of youths. If a youth is accused of a crime, for example, courts often order evaluations to identify psychopathological and attitudinal factors that should be considered in the disposition of the case. Although accused youths are apt to deny aggressive and delinquent behavior on the YSR, the degree to which they acknowledge externalizing behaviors that are known to occur can serve as an index of their general candor.

The internalizing problems that youths report on the YSR can indicate whether they acknowledge enough inner discomfort—such as on the YSR Anxious/Depressed scale—to be motivated for personal help. The Thought Problems scale can indicate whether deficient reality testing may be involved, while the Social Problems scale can indicate feelings of rejection by peers. Specific items such as *18. I deliberately try to hurt or kill myself* and *91. I think about killing myself* are also important to examine for danger signs.

Another forensic use of the YSR is to evaluate youths after stressful experiences, such as sex abuse or family disruption. It can also be used in evaluations for placement decisions necessitated by custody disputes between parents and by state intervention to terminate parental rights. In these contexts, the YSR can aid in determining the degree and type of deviance expressed by the youth that should be considered in making dispositions and in evaluating reports by others about the youth. After a disposition has been made, such as placement with one of the parents, a foster home, or group home, the YSR and related instruments can be repeated periodically to monitor the youth's progress.

DIAGNOSTIC ISSUES

As discussed earlier, special educational services usually require justification according to administrative categories, such as those prescribed by P.L.94-142. Diagnostic classification systems, such as DSM-III-R (American Psychiatric Association, 1987), often serve an analogous function for purposes of third party reimbursement for services. For purposes of record keeping and billing, it is usually necessary to assign each case to one or more official diagnostic categories. Although the concept of diagnosis also implies comprehensive case formulations, the DSM-III-R categories of child/youth disorders do not constitute detailed formulations. Instead, they are defined largely by lists of descriptive features and rules specifying the number of features required to meet the criterion for each diagnosis.

The DSM criteria are conventions formulated by committees. These conventions are subject to change, as illustrated by the substantial changes from the DSM-III to the DSM-III-R categories of child/youth disorders and in the defining criteria for the categories that have survived. Although it is hoped that different causes will ultimately be found to underlie the different categories of disorders, it is not known whether the DSM child/youth categories actually reflect underlying differences.

Many youths manifest features of multiple DSM categories, rather than fitting neatly into single categories. It is therefore important to base help on accurate assessment of all their needs, instead of viewing them only in terms of diagnostic categories.

The instruments we have developed provide a differentiated picture of problems and competencies as they are seen from different perspectives, rather than forcing them into predetermined categories. Nevertheless, the empirically based syndromes and scores are highly relevant to diagnostic classifications, as well as to more comprehensive diagnostic formulations. Several of the syndromes derived empirically from our instruments have approximate counterparts in the DSM-III-R, as summarized in Table 9-2. These relations concern similarities in descriptive features, although efforts to operationalize assessment of DSM diagnostic categories have also confirmed significant statistical associations with the empirically derived YSR syndromes (Weinstein, Noam, Grimes, Stone, & Schwab-Stone, 1990), as well as with CBCL and TRF syndromes (Edelbrock & Costello, 1988; Edelbrock, Costello, & Kessler, 1984). In making DSM diagnoses, scores in the clinical range on the empirically derived syndromes would argue in favor of the corresponding DSM diagnoses listed in the left-hand column of Table 9-2.

Because neither diagnostic formulations nor formal diagnoses should be based on a single source of data, the diagnostic process requires coordination of data from multiple sources, such as parent-reports, teacher-reports, interviews, tests, observations, and physical exams. If a youth is in the clinical range on similar syndrome scales scored from the YSR, CBCL, TRF, and/or DOF, this would argue for a diagnosis corresponding to such syndromes. Because there may be complex variations among the data obtained from multiple sources, the *Integrative Guide* (Achenbach, 1991a) provides various procedures for using multisource data in the diagnostic process.

PLANNING AND ACCOUNTABILITY FOR SERVICES

With increasing emphasis on planning and accountability for services, it is important to document the types of problems for which services are needed and the effects of the services on the problems.

Table 9-2

Approximate Relations Between DSM-III-R and the CBCL, YSR, TRF, and DOF Syndromes

DSM-III-R	CBCL	YSR	TRF	DOF
Avoidant Disorder	Withdrawn	Withdrawn	Withdrawn	Withdrawn-Inattentive
Somatization Disorder	Somatic Complaints	Somatic Complaints	Somatic Complaints	—
Overanxious Disorder	Anxious/Depressed	Anxious/Depressed	Anxious/Depressed	Nervous-Obsessive
Major Depression	"	"	"	Depressed
Dysthymia	"	"	"	"
Schizotypal Personality	Thought Problems	Thought Problems	Thought Problems	—
Psychotic Disorders	"	"	"	
Attention Deficit-Hyperactivity Disorder	Attention Problems	Attention Problems	Attention Problems	Hyperactive
Group Delinquent Conduct Disorder	Delinquent Behavior	Delinquent Behavior	Delinquent Behavior	—
Solitary Aggressive Conduct Disorder	Aggressive Behavior	Aggressive Behavior	Aggressive Behavior	Aggressive Behavior
Oppositional Defiant Disorder	"	"	"	"
Gender Identity Disorder for Males	Sex Problems[a]	Self-Destructive/Identity Problems[b]	—	—

[a]Scored for ages 4-11 only. See CBCL Manual (Achenbach, 1991b). [b]Scored for boys only.

Needs Assessment

To determine the number of youths in a particular population who are likely to need help for behavioral/emotional problems, randomly selected members of the population can be surveyed by having them complete the YSR anonymously. If the target youths can be reached through schools or other group settings, it may often be easier to have them all fill out YSRs at the same time, rather than arranging for randomly-selected subsamples to fill out YSRs. Obtaining YSRs for all members of a population also has the advantage of providing more accurate prevalence data than can be obtained from subsamples, especially for relatively uncommon problems.

YSR survey data can be used to determine the number of youths in the population who have total scores in the clinical range and the number who show marked deviance in particular areas, as indicated by high scores on particular syndrome scales, such as the Anxious/Depressed or Aggressive Behavior scales. The proportion reporting specific problems—such as suicidal thoughts—can also be assessed by tabulating individual items. More differentiated analyses of the population can be made by determining the proportion of particular subgroups who show the highest rates of particular problems. If the target population consists of pupils in a school system, for example, comparisons can be made between boys and girls, different ethnic groups, younger versus older pupils, different schools, and students enrolled in different curricula, such as general versus college preparatory.

Accountability for Services

The YSR can contribute to accountability by having each referred youth complete it as part of the initial assessment process. The YSR and its profile can then become part of the youth's clinical record and can be used in conjunction with profiles from other informants in planning services. Thereafter, the YSR and other instruments can be readministered to monitor the progress and outcome of services. If improvement is not found, a change in the treatment should be considered. This general model can be employed for outpatient mental health services, inpatient and residential services, foster home placement, group homes, and school-based services.

Beside providing accountability for individual cases, the YSR can also provide accountability at the level of programs and variations within programs. The data obtained with the YSR across a defined period, such as a year, can be used to document the number of cases having particular types of problems, the degree of deviance in the cases served, the relations of particular problems to demographic variables, and the disposition of cases having particular problems. Such data are important for reporting clinical activities, justifying requests for funding, and program planning.

If a clinical service offers a variety of treatment modalities, the YSR can be used as one basis for assigning youths to the different modalities. Youths whose YSR profiles show deviance mainly on internalizing scales, for example, might be assigned to talking therapies. Those who show deviance mainly on externalizing scales, by contrast, might be assigned to drug, behavioral, or milieu therapies. By reassessing the youths periodically, we can determine whether the outcomes for each group are favorable after receiving their respective treatment modalities.

We can also determine whether particular internalizing, mixed, or externalizing profile patterns, or particular problems or scale scores are related to especially poor outcomes. If so, this would indicate that better interventions need to be found for youths with these characteristics, either by assigning them to different treatment options than previously, by developing new interventions tailored more specifically to their needs, or by referring them to settings that might be more effective with them.

Case Registers

At the level of catchment areas or county or state mental health systems, the YSR, CBCL, and TRF can provide the basis for *case registers* that are designed to obtain standardized data on all cases seen in a designated area. When maintained over an extended period, such as a year, a case register provides valuable data on the number of cases having each kind of problem, differences between the problems seen in different facilities, associations of particular problems with variables such as ethnicity and socioeconomic status, seasonal fluctuations, etc.

Our microcomputer programs enable each participating agency to score all forms for its own use and to send diskettes of data to a central facility for aggregation across the entire area served by the case register. No names need to be transmitted, as each agency can use its own code numbers. Each agency can also print profiles and retain computer files of YSR data for its own use.

If regular follow-ups are done for each clinical service (e.g., at 6-month intervals), the follow-up data can be analyzed to determine the progress of cases seen in the designated area. Follow-up data on the course of particular kinds of problems and cases can aid in planning and justifying agency budgets by answering the frequently asked question, "What happens to these kids later?"

TRAINING OF PRACTITIONERS

The YSR can contribute to various aspects of training, as exemplified in the following sections.

Training for Intake Assessments

If trainees are taught to use the YSR as part of the initial assessment, they can learn to use interviews to follow up on the youths' YSR responses and to focus on matters better dealt with in interviews. Interviewing is costly, as it requires an appointment system, waiting and interview rooms, advance preparation, and the practitioner's time to conduct the interview and compile the interview data. Costs are further increased by the occasional failure of clients to keep appointments. Training of interview skills is still more costly, because cases must be selected for their training value and both the supervisor and trainee must be involved. It is therefore important to make the best possible use of the time for training interviewers, rather than wasting time to get information that can be obtained more economically and efficiently with the YSR.

Selecting Teaching Cases

The lack of a well-validated diagnostic system for adolescent disorders makes it hard to select cases that clearly exemplify particular disorders. Extensive assessment is required to determine whether a youth truly fits diagnostic categories like those of the DSM. Even when a youth does meet the criteria for a DSM diagnosis, viewing the youth solely in terms of a diagnostic category may obscure other important facets of the case. The YSR can therefore be helpful in selecting cases that illustrate complex patterns not adequately subsumed by DSM categories.

Comparing Data from Different Sources

A key objective of training is to help trainees grasp the multifaceted and relativistic nature of young people's problems and competencies. The YSR can be used to compare and contrast behavior reported by youths on the YSR versus in interviews. It can also be used to compare the youth's self-reports with reports obtained on the CBCL, TRF, and/or DOF. This can help the trainee form a more comprehensive picture of the youth than by soliciting unstructured descriptions. It can also pinpoint discrepancies that need exploration to determine whether they reflect differences in the youth's behavior in different situations or idiosyncracies of the informants' reports.

SUMMARY

This chapter addressed applications of the YSR to making practical decisions about particular cases, groups, programs, policies, etc. The YSR provides standardized descriptive data for comparison with normative samples of peers seen from the perspectives of different informants.

Applications in mental health contexts were illustrated in relation to intake and evaluation, clinical interviewing, planning, interventions, and reassessments.

Applications in school contexts were illustrated in relation to referral for special education services, assessment, and determination of eligibility for special education under Public Law 94-142. Protection of the confidentiality of YSR responses is especially important in school settings.

Applications in medical contexts include routine use by medical providers to identify behavioral/emotional problems and also to provide reassurance when such problems are in the normal range. Assessment of concomitant behavioral/ emotional problems is especially important for youths who have serious physical illnesses or handicaps.

Forensic applications include evaluations of youths implicated in crime, evaluations of problems following traumatic experiences, evaluation for placement decisions, and following placement.

Special education services, record keeping, and third party reimbursement for clinical services usually require assigning cases to administrative or diagnostic categories. Tables were provided that summarize descriptive similarities between the empirically derived syndromes of the YSR, CBCL, TRF, and DOF and the criteria for P.L. 94-142 special education categories, as well as for DSM diagnostic categories. Deviant scores on the syndrome scales can be used as evidence in favor of the corresponding special education and diagnostic categories.

It is increasingly important to document the types of problems for which services are needed and the effects of services on the problems. The YSR can be used in needs assessments, assessments of the problems and outcomes in particular caseloads, and case registers for obtaining standardized data on all cases seen in a designated area.

The YSR can contribute to the training of practitioners by teaching them to combine standardized rating data with interviews, economically selecting teaching cases, and comparing similar standardized data from multiple sources.

Chapter 10
Research Use of
the YSR and Profile

Chapter 9 outlined some ways in which the YSR can be used for assessment on which to base practical decisions about particular cases and situations. The YSR, its scales, and profile are products of research designed to improve our ways of helping young people. Much remains to be learned, however, and the YSR can be used in many ways to expand our knowledge through research.

The *Integrative Guide* (Achenbach, 1991a) focuses on multiaxial aspects of research involving the YSR, CBCL, and TRF. Because agreement between different informants may not be very high, it is desirable to obtain data from multiple sources whenever possible. However, for many purposes, research may center on youths' reports in particular, or youths may happen to be the most feasible and appropriate sources of data. This chapter therefore focuses primarily on research use of the YSR, although self-reports should be viewed as only one component of comprehensive assessment. The topics generally parallel those presented in the *Integrative Guide*, but with variations specific to the YSR.

Use of the YSR is not confined to any single theoretical view, topic, or type of research. Instead, the YSR provides an assessment procedure and data language that can be shared by workers differing in theoretical persuasions and research interests. Furthermore, the YSR can be used in conjunction with many other sources of data, such as tests, parents' reports, interviews, direct observations, teachers' reports, biomedical procedures, and life histories.

Research on a particular type of disorder, such as depression or aggression, typically employs measures specific to that type of disorder. Because the YSR has eight syndrome scales, it can be used to assess disorders corresponding to any of these eight scales. Even if a more specialized procedure is used to assess a particular type of disorder, the inclusion of the YSR can reveal problems in other areas that may be equally as important. In research on aggression, for example, both the YSR and a specialized measure of aggression may identify subjects who obtain high scores for aggression. However, the instrument that measures only aggression will fail to distinguish youth who report only aggressive problems from those who would also report significant problems in other areas, if they were asked. The YSR, by contrast, is designed to simultaneously obtain reports of problems and competencies in many areas in addition to aggression. For research on a particular disorder, such as aggression, the YSR would thus be useful for distinguishing between youths who report problems only in the area of the target disorder and those who present more complex pictures that cannot be discerned via measures that assess only the target disorder.

This chapter first deals with questions arising in the use of raw scores versus *T* scores for the YSR scales and in analyzing scores across both sexes. Thereafter, it describes applications to research areas including epidemiology, diagnosis, etiology, services, outcomes, medical conditions, and cross-cultural comparisons. Because creative research blends ideas, opportunities, and methods in new ways, readers will no doubt think of many research possibilities beside those mentioned here. To facilitate access to research possibilities and findings, our *Bibliography of Published Studies Using the Child Behavior and Related Materials* is updated annually. The 1991 edition lists some 200 topics dealt with in over 700 publications (Achenbach & Brown, 1991). Table 10-1 lists examples of research topics for which the YSR has been used in studies listed in the *Bibliography*.

Table 10-1
Examples of Research Topics for
which the YSR has been Used[a]

Children of alcoholics	Hormonal factors
Comparisons with parent- and teacher-reports	Inpatients
	Mother/daughter perspectives
Cross-cultural comparisons	Oppositional disorder
Custody	Risk factors for problems
Depression	Self-concept
Diabetes	Social-emotional adjustment
DSM diagnoses	Stressful events
DSM-Psychosocial Axis	Suicide
Gender problems	Temperament
Headaches	Visually handicapped youths

[a]Topics for which studies employing the YSR are listed in the *Bibliography of Published Studies Using the Child Behavior Checklist and Related Materials: 1991 Edition* (Achenbach & Brown, 1991).

USE OF RAW SCORES VERSUS T SCORES IN RESEARCH WITH THE YSR

Chapters 2 and 3 described the computation of raw scale scores and the assignment of T scores to the YSR scales. The main function of the T scores is to facilitate comparisons of the degree of deviance indicated by respondents' standing on different scales and different instruments. A T score of 70, for example, indicates that a youth scored at approximately the 98th percentile of our normative sample for youths of that sex. Because the T scores from 50 to 70 were similarly based on percentiles for the syndrome scales of the YSR, a youth who obtains a T score of 70 on the YSR Aggressive Behavior scale and 55 on the YSR Somatic Complaints scale is more deviant in reported aggression than in somatic problems, relative to norms based on self-reports.

Suppose that the youth who obtained a T score of 70 on the YSR Aggressive Behavior scale obtained a T score of 50 on the

TRF Aggressive Behavior scale. This indicates that the youth's teacher reported much less aggressive behavior, relative to reports by teachers in our normative sample, than did the youth, relative to self-reports by peers in our normative sample.

By being based on percentiles for the normative sample, the T scores provide a convenient way of quickly judging whether a youth reports relatively many or few competencies and problems, as compared to nonreferred peers. However, because the distributions of scale scores vary among samples, and because of our method for assigning T scores at the extremes of the distributions, the T scores do not provide a perfectly uniform index of deviance. Furthermore, because we truncated the assignment of T scores at the nondeviant end of the syndrome and competence scales, raw scores can reflect greater differentiation among nondeviant subjects than T scores can on these scales. This is not the case for the total competence, Internalizing, Externalizing, and total problem scores, however, where the T scores were not truncated.

Statistical Analysis of Scale Scores

For statistical analysis of the competence and syndrome scales, it is usually preferable to use the raw scale scores rather than the T scores in order to take account of the full range of variation in these scales. Because T scores were not truncated for the total competence, Internalizing, Externalizing, and total problem scores, statistical analyses using the T scores for these scales should yield results similar to those using the raw scores. In any case, the actual distributions of scores to be analyzed should be checked for compatibility with the statistics to be used. If the obtained distributions depart much from the statistical assumptions, other statistical procedures or transformations of the scores may be needed.

If a researcher wishes to compare a particular sample with our YSR normative samples, the simplest way is to compare the mean and standard deviation of the sample's raw scores with the mean and standard deviation of the raw scores shown in Table 3-3 for the corresponding normative sample. Because any particular research sample is selected differently than our normative sample, the means and standard deviations are likely to differ between the samples. However, the researcher can determine whether the research sample's scores are similar to, much higher, or much lower than those of our normative sample. Similar comparisons can be made with the scores shown in Appendix B for our demographically matched referred and nonreferred samples.

The truncation, normalizing transformation, and equal-interval assignment of extreme T scores in our normative samples make direct comparisons with T scores from a particular research sample more tenuous than comparisons of raw scores. However, if a researcher wishes to describe a sample in terms of our T scores, all the raw scores in the sample should first be individually converted to T scores, as is done by our YSR computer program. The mean and standard deviation of these T scores can then be compared with the mean and standard deviation of the T scores reported for our normative sample in Table 3-3 or clinical sample in Appendix B. The mean and standard deviation of a raw score distribution should *not* be converted directly to the equivalent T scores shown on the YSR profile, because this wrongly assumes that the raw score and T score distributions have identical shapes.

RESEARCH INCLUDING BOTH SEXES

By using a common set of eight syndrome scales for the 1991 YSR boys' and girls' profiles, we have designed the profiles to facilitate comparisons between both sexes. A ninth syndrome, Self-Destructive/Identity Problems, is scored only for boys. Because it is specific to boys on the YSR, the Self-Destructive/Identity Problems syndrome is not displayed as a scale on the profile, although the computer-scoring program and hand-scoring profiles display raw scores and T scores. The Internalizing, Externalizing, and total problem scales comprise the same items for both sexes, while the competence scales are also uniform for both sexes. To take account of sex differences in scores, percentiles and T scores were based on separate normative samples of each sex. This makes it possible to compare a youth's score on any scale with a normative group of the same sex.

If statistical analyses are to be done on samples that include youths of both sexes, the sex differences in scores must be taken into account. On some scales, a particular raw score may represent a different degree of deviance in one sex than in the other. For example, a raw score of 15 is just below the clinical cutpoint on the Anxious/Depressed scale for girls, but is above the clinical cutpoint for boys. If we compare the raw scores of two samples that differ greatly in the proportion of girls versus boys, the sample having more girls might appear more deviant. However, because the normative base rate for the problems of the Anxious/Depressed scale is higher for girls than for boys, this would be a misleading conclusion.

To prevent sex differences from being confounded with other variables, several options are available. For analyses of the Internalizing, Externalizing, total problem, and total competence scores that include both sexes, the T scores for each sex can be used. These T scores reflect each subject's deviation from the mean of his/her normative group without losing any of the differentiation that is lost by truncating T scores, as occurs on some of the syndrome and competence scales.

For syndrome and competence scales that have only one raw score assigned to the truncated T score ($T = 50$ on syndrome scales, $T = 55$ on competence scales), the T scores can be used without any loss of differentiation. For syndrome scales that have multiple raw scores assigned to $T = 50$, the loss of differentiation incurred by using T scores will depend on how many different scores in a research sample would be assigned $T = 50$.

As an example, the Aggressive Behavior scale for boys assigns $T = 50$ to raw scores of 0 to 8. If many boys in a research sample obtain raw scores of 0 to 8, use of T scores is apt to yield less statistical power than use of raw scores. However, since all scores receiving $T = 50$ are at the low end of the normal range, a researcher may decide that the differences among such scores merely add "noise" to analyses of clinically important variables. The researcher might therefore use T scores to reduce the differentiation among low normal raw scores. On the other hand, if a researcher wishes to preserve all the differentiation in raw scores analyzed for both sexes, then the raw scores can be converted to z scores within the sample of each sex.

EPIDEMIOLOGICAL RESEARCH

Epidemiology is the study of the rate and distribution of disorders in populations. It is especially concerned with the *incidence* (rate of onset) of new disorders, and the *prevalence* (percent of the population having disorders) at particular points in time. Knowledge of the incidence, prevalence, and distribution of disorders is important for planning services, developing hypotheses about causal factors, identifying changes in rates over time, and interpreting findings on particular research samples in light of data from samples of large populations. For instruments such as the YSR, epidemiological data are also needed to provide normative distributions of scores on which to base cutpoints for discriminating between the normal and clinical range.

Population Studies

Population studies are typically designed to estimate the prevalence of disorders or problems in a large population at a particular point in time. The target population can be defined as all the youths between certain ages living in a particular geographical area, such as a city, county, state, region, or country. Because it is seldom feasible to assess every youth in the target population, samples of youths are assessed as a basis for estimating prevalence rates in the entire population. The sampling procedures must be carefully designed to obtain samples that are as representative as possible of the population. That is, every youth in the population must have an equal chance of being selected for assessment. However, it is not only the sampling procedure, but completion rates in the selected sample and the quality of the assessment procedures that determine whether the obtained data validly represent the entire population.

For population studies of behavioral/emotional problems among adolescents, the subjects themselves are important sources of data. To maximize our chance of obtaining representative self-report data, it is necessary to use standardized assessment procedures that are economical, acceptable to youths, easy to administer, brief, reliable, and efficiently scored. To maximize the utility of the data, the instruments should not be narrowly restricted to predetermined concepts of disorders that are apt to change. The instruments should also be usable in a similar fashion with different kinds samples, such as clinical criterion groups.

The YSR was designed to meet all the foregoing requirements, and it has been used in population studies in several cultures (e.g., Achenbach & Edelbrock, 1987; Achenbach, Bird, Canino, Phares, Gould, & Rubio-Stipec, 1990; Köferl, 1988; Remschmidt & Walter, 1989; Verhulst, Prince, Vervuurt-Poot, & deJong, 1989). The methodology used in these studies can be applied to population samples almost anywhere.

Data obtained in new studies using the same methodology can be rigorously compared with data obtained in the previous studies to identify similarities and differences between populations and from one time to another within a population. Population studies in particular areas can also be used to determine base rates for self-reported problems and competencies in those areas. Comparisons can be made to determine whether rates differ for particular groups within an area, such as youths from certain neighborhoods or ethnic groups, or disadvantaged or handicapped youths. Mental health agencies may wish to establish local norms for their catchment areas to use as a baseline with which to compare youths referred for services.

Case Registers

Research on individuals who are referred for services provides an important complement to population-based studies. Individual clinical services, however, are subject to biases in their caseloads, owing to their specific locations, referral sources that channel cases to one service versus another, admission requirements, economic factors, service philosophies, and the images that they project to consumers. As a consequence, no one service is likely to provide a representative sample of referred youths within an area, unless it is the sole service in that area.

Case registers for recording uniform data on all cases referred for services within a delimited area can be extremely valuable for obtaining clinical samples that are less biased than those of any single service. By obtaining data from multiple services, case registers can also yield larger samples of uncommon disorders than can single facilities or general population samples. Furthermore, the variations in cases across multiple services can enable researchers to test associations between disorders and a wider range of case characteristics than in single facilities. Case registers of infectious diseases, for example, provide data on SES, ethnic, age, sex, occupational, and secular variations in the diseases. These data are used to develop hypotheses about etiologies and outcomes.

A comprehensive case register for adolescent psychopathology would include youths referred to special education services and juvenile courts, as well as those referred for mental health services, because all three kinds of services deal with an overlapping range of problems. The YSR can be requested as part of the evaluation process in all services participating in a case register. The register would be designed to obtain other kinds of data according to the aims of the researchers and what can feasibly be obtained in all the participating services. The value of a register can be enhanced by including systematic follow-ups of cases in order to study the course and outcomes of disorders in association with other variables, such as initial case characteristics and type of service received. If the amount and cost of services can be accurately recorded for all cases, case registers can also enable researchers to study the cost of caring for cases that are classified according to the problems reported on the initial YSR.

DIAGNOSTIC AND TAXONOMIC RESEARCH

To validly distinguish among disorders, a diagnostic system requires a *taxonomy* for grouping disorders according to their distinguishing features. It also requires *assessment procedures* for identifying the features of each case that correspond to the taxonomic groupings. A comprehensive approach to the taxonomic basis for diagnosis should include multiple assessment procedures that converge on the taxonomic groupings from different angles. The *Integrative Guide* (Achenbach, 1991a) discusses coordination of the YSR, CBCL, and TRF in efforts to improve the taxonomic basis for diagnosis of childhood disorders. Because self-reports are important for evaluating clinically referred youths, the YSR can be a key element in diagnostic and taxonomic research.

The eight cross-informant syndromes provide a basis for taxonomy of many adolescent problems. One approach to research is to test the correspondence between the YSR scores on the eight syndromes and assessment data obtained via other systems based on data from youths. As an example, Weinstein et al. (1990) analyzed associations between pre-1991 YSR syndrome scores and DSM-III diagnoses made for adolescent inpatients from the Diagnostic Interview Schedule for Children (DISC). Significant associations were found between DISC diagnoses and the corresponding syndromes of the YSR.

Because youths are important sources of data for diagnoses made from subsequent editions of the DSM, it would be worth testing the associations between the 1991 YSR syndromes and current versions of DSM diagnoses made from self-reports. For those DSM disorders that are defined by multiple descriptive features, the number of features that youths report to be present can be summed to provide a quantitative score for each DSM disorder. By testing both this quantitative score and various cutpoints on the score, the researcher can determine whether the standard criteria for DSM diagnoses, other cutpoints, or continuous quantitative scores provide better agreement with the YSR syndrome scores. Conversely, the YSR quantitative scores can be compared with various cutpoints on the scores to identify the best basis for agreement with DSM diagnoses.

It should be noted that the cutpoints which maximize agreement between different assessment procedures and different taxonomic criteria may be specific to particular samples. A sample that includes many high scores, for example, may benefit from a higher cutpoint than a sample with few high scores. For cutpoints to be generalizable, it is therefore necessary to use samples that are representative of large populations and/or to compare the effects of particular cutpoints when they are applied to samples that differ in important ways. The *Integrative Guide* (Achenbach, 1991a) outlines additional ways in which the YSR can be used for diagnostic and taxonomic research in conjunction with the CBCL, TRF, and other procedures.

ETIOLOGICAL RESEARCH

Etiological research aims to identify the causes of disorders. The behavioral/emotional disorders of adolescence are likely to involve many different kinds of causal factors, such as genetic, temperamental, interactions with parents, traumatic, and cultural. Some factors may not ordinarily be causal in themselves, but may raise the risk of behavioral/emotional problems under particular conditions. Youths who are cognitively either much more or less advanced than their peers, for example, may face frustrations that spawn behavioral/emotional problems, even though there is nothing pathological about their cognitive functioning per se.

Because the determinants of behavioral/emotional disorders are likely to be complex, it is important to triangulate multiple variables from multiple perspectives. The multiaxial model that was presented in Table 1-1 is therefore relevant to etiological research as well as to clinical assessment of individual youths. The *Integrative Guide* outlines approaches to coordinating the YSR, CBCL, and TRF in etiological research. It is recommended that etiological research employ assessment from these different perspectives whenever possible, as well as from other perspectives, such as observations, interviews, tests, laboratory measures, and biomedical assays. For some purposes, however, self-reports may be the main source of data about behavior and emotions.

Examples of etiological research using the YSR include the following:

1. Identify youths who all manifest a particular YSR profile pattern and compare them with youths who manifest a different profile pattern with respect to hypothesized differences in etiology.

2. Group youths whose highest score is on one scale—such as the Anxious/Depressed Scale—for comparison with those whose score is on a different scale, such as the Withdrawn scale.

3. If a potential etiological factor, such as a particular type of traumatic experience, can be identified, compare YSR scores and profile patterns for subjects who do and do not have the etiological factor to determine whether they differ in self-reported behavioral/emotional problems. If they do differ, this would be evidence in favor of a causal role for the identified etiological factor.

4. If hypothesized etiological factors can be experimentally manipulated, the YSR can be completed following different experimental conditions to determine whether self-reported problems change in response to the manipulations. If it is hypothesized that a particular drug alleviates an organic abnormality, for example, YSRs could be completed after a 2-month period when the subjects receive the drug and also after a 2-month period when they receive a placebo. The experimental order should be counterbalanced so that some youths receive one condition first, while others receive the other condition first. To use the YSR for assessment periods shorter than the usual 6-month period, the instructions need only be changed to specify the target period. Scores obtained at the end of each experimental condition would then be compared to determine whether they differ significantly.

OUTCOME RESEARCH

If we knew the typical outcome for each childhood disorder following no intervention and following each of several intervention options, we would be in a much better position to make decisions about individual cases. Furthermore, if types of cases were identified that typically had poor outcomes following all available interventions as well as following no intervention, these types of cases should receive high priority for research designed to improve interventions. Self-reports are a prime source of baseline data with which to compare outcomes. Because the YSR is scored on the same syndrome scales from age 11 to 18, it offers exceptional continuity of assessment for studies of adolescent outcomes, over periods ranging from a few months to 7 years. Furthermore, the YSR scores and profile patterns obtained at the initial assessment can be tested as potential predictors of outcome.

If we find that particular YSR scores or profile patterns are typically followed by much worse outcomes than other scores or patterns, then new cases manifesting the prognosticators of poor outcomes can be selected for research efforts to improve their outcomes. Other variables, such as teacher- and parent-ratings, interview data, family constellation, cognitive measures, and biomedical conditions, might also be found to augment predictions of outcomes. These variables could then be used in conjunction with the YSR to identify cases expected to have poor outcomes and to develop better ways of helping them.

Just as additional variables may augment prediction of outcomes from initial characteristics, the outcomes themselves should be evaluated using criteria in addition to the YSR whenever possible. The additional criteria could include teacher- and parent-ratings obtainable with the TRF and CBCL, cognitive functioning, new problems, referral for various services, etc.

Groups at Risk

Beside testing predictions of outcomes from subject variables, outcome research can be useful for determining the relative risk rates for youths thought to be predisposed to poor outcomes by certain identifiable background conditions. Youths whose family members are alcoholic, schizophrenic, or depressed, for example, are thought to be at elevated risk for behavioral/emotional problems. To determine whether such youths have elevated rates of problems in general or the specific problems tapped by particular syndrome scales, YSRs could be compared from each of several risk groups and youths not having any of the risk factors. However, it would also be important to obtain data from other informants as well, such as teachers.

EXPERIMENTAL INTERVENTION STUDIES

If outcome research identifies case characteristics that predict poor outcomes, this argues for active efforts to improve outcomes for these cases. The most rigorous way to determine whether a particular intervention can improve outcomes is to experimentally manipulate the intervention conditions. Experimental studies require a large enough supply of appropriate cases to be assigned to different experimental conditions, such as by randomized assignment to Intervention A versus Intervention B versus no intervention. For some types of interventions, such as drugs or contingency manipulations designed to alter specific behaviors, it may be possible to test each intervention with the same subjects receiving both interventions in counterbalanced sequences, such as ABAB and BABA.

Suppose that an outcome study showed that youths scoring high on the YSR Anxious/Depressed and Aggressive Behavior scales had especially poor outcomes. Suppose that we therefore develop Intervention A designed for this group and wish to determine whether it yields better results than Intervention B or no intervention.

The YSR can be employed in several ways to test whether Intervention A is better than Intervention B or no intervention. First, because the youths to be tested are those with high scores on the YSR Anxious/Depressed and Aggressive Behavior scales, the YSR is used to identify subjects for the study. Because all the subjects fill out the YSR prior to the intervention conditions, it provides a baseline measure against which to compare outcomes. After intervention, all the youths are asked to fill out the YSR again. The postintervention scores can then be compared with preintervention scores for each intervention condition. Other measures, such as parent and teacher ratings, should also be used.

Beside being used to select subjects and to assess the effects of interventions, the YSR can be used to create matched groups to receive different intervention conditions. In a *randomized blocks design*, for example, subgroups of subjects (called "blocks") are first matched with respect to YSR scores and other important variables, such as age, sex, and SES. The members of a block are then randomly assigned to the different intervention conditions. If there are three intervention conditions, each member of a block of subjects is randomly assigned to a different one of the three conditions. If the interventions can be varied for the same individuals—such as an active drug alternated with a placebo—matched groups can be formed to receive the interventions in different orders. Some subjects thus receive the drug first followed by the placebo. Other subjects matched to them for YSR scores and other characteristics receive the opposite order.

STUDIES OF DIAGNOSTIC CONSTRUCTS

The YSR can be used in studies of particular diagnostic constructs. If we wish to study depression as a diagnostic construct, for example, high scores on the YSR Anxious/ Depressed scale can be used as one criterion for selecting depressed youths, while low scores on the Anxious/Depressed scale are used for selecting a nondepressed comparison group. Other measures designed specifically to assess depression as a diagnostic construct could also be used. A multidimensional measure such as the YSR has the advantage of showing whether a youth reports problems only in the target area or in other areas as well. If we measure only one syndrome, we will not know whether a youth who is deviant in that syndrome is also deviant in other areas. To form groups who are relatively "pure" with respect to a particular diagnostic construct, it is important to insure that they are not too heterogeneous with respect to other types of problems.

ABUSED YOUTHS

Beside the syndromes yielded by our analyses of the YSR, other groups of items may be consistently related to particular types of problems. If YSRs are completed by youths known to have a particular type of problem, they can be compared with YSRs completed by youths not having that problem to determine whether there are consistent differences. YSRs completed by abused youths, for example, can be compared with those completed by demographically similar nonabused youths. Because abuse may be associated with a variety of behavioral/emotional problems, it would be advisable to compare abused youths with clinically referred nonabused youths, as well as with normal youths. By including a clinical comparison group, we can determine whether there are particular items that distinguish abused youths from those distressed for other reasons. If particular items are found to distinguish youths who have a type of problem not directly assessed by the YSR, such as abuse, the YSR can then be used as an aid in identifying new cases having this type of problem. The YSR can also be used in conjunction with other assessment procedures to study the progress of abused youths receiving different intervention conditions, such as individual therapy, family therapy, or foster placement.

RESEARCH ON MEDICAL CONDITIONS

Certain behavioral/emotional problems may accompany particular medical conditions. In some cases, a medical condition or a medical treatment may specifically cause problems such as inattention, motor tics, depression, lethargy, or overactivity. In other cases, a medical condition may cause stress that raises the risk of behavioral/emotional problems. To determine whether particular behavioral/emotional problems tend to accompany particular medical conditions, the YSR can be used to compare youths having each medical condition with youths having other medical conditions and with physically healthy youths. The comparisons between youths having different medical conditions are helpful for avoiding erroneous attributions of elevated rates of problems to a particular condition, when they may actually accompany multiple conditions.

The YSR can be used as an outcome measure in interventions aimed at reducing behavioral/emotional problems associated with medical conditions. Afflicted youths can be assessed with the YSR before and after receiving a particular intervention versus a control condition to determine whether the youths have fewer behavioral/emotional problems after the intervention than after the control condition. To illustrate the range of possibilities for using the YSR in research on medical conditions, Table 10-2 summarizes medically related topics from the *Bibliography of Published Studies Using the Child Behavior Checklist and Related Materials* (Achenbach & Brown, 1991).

Table 10-2
Examples of Medical Conditions for Which
Research has Employed the CBCL, YSR, or TRF[a]

Abdominal pain	Hearing impairment	Obesity
Adrenal hyperplasia	Hemophilia	Pain
Arthritis	Hermaphro-ditism	Phenyl-ketonuria
Asphyxia	Hypospadias	Precocious puberty
Asthma	Hypo-thyroidism	Reyes syndrome
Birth defects	Language disorders	Short stature
Brain damage	Lead toxicity	Sickle cell anemia
Cancer	Leukemia	Sleep disturbance
Cerebral palsy	Limb deficiency	Spina bifida
Cleft palate	Low birthweight	Tourette's syndrome
Colitis	Meningitis	Trauma
Crohn's disease	Mental retardation	Tracheostomy
Cystic fibrosis	Migraine	Turner's syndrome
Diabetes	Neuro-pathology	Visual impairment
Ear disease		
Epilepsy		
Epstein-Barr virus		
Headaches		

[a]From Achenbach & Brown (1991) *Bibliography of Published Studies Using the Child Behavior Checklist and Related Materials: 1991 Edition.*

CROSS-CULTURAL RESEARCH

To advance the study of psychopathology, it is important to calibrate assessment procedures across different countries and cultures. If similar procedures produce similar results in different cultures, this supports the cross-cultural robustness of the findings and the possibilities for integrating results from the different cultures. If different results are obtained from different cultures, by contrast, the findings may provide clues as to causal factors related to the cultural differences.

The YSR has been used in studies outside the United States, including epidemiological comparisons with prevalence rates of problems in Germany (Köferl, 1988; Remschmidt & Walter, 1989), Holland (Verhulst et al., 1989), and Puerto Rico (Achenbach, Bird, et al., 1990). The factor structure of the YSR obtained for American youths has also been compared with the factor structure obtained for German youths (Köferl, 1988). At this writing, we know of translations of the CBCL or its related forms into the 33 languages listed in Table 10-3. The *Bibliography* (Achenbach & Brown, 1991) lists published studies in 15 cultures. The YSR has also been translated into several of the languages listed in Table 10-3 and could readily be adapted from the CBCL translations in others.

General population epidemiological studies in Holland and Puerto Rico have yielded lower YSR problem scores than found in our United States samples (Achenbach et al., 1990; Verhulst et al, 1989), although Australian (Sawyer, 1990) and German (Köferl, 1988) YSR scores have been more similar to American scores. The Dutch and Puerto Rican YSR scores contrast with CBCL and TRF scores for the same samples, in that the Dutch CBCL and TRF scores were quite similar to ours but the Puerto Rican scores were much higher than ours. It is not clear why American youth report so many more problems than their parents and teachers, as well as more than their Dutch and Puerto Rican counterparts. The tendency of

Table 10-3
Translations of the CBCL, YSR, and/or TRF

Afrikaans	Korean
Amharic	Norwegian
(Ethiopia)	Papiamento-Aruba
Arabic	Papiamento-Curacao
Bengali	Portuguese
Cambodian	Portuguese Creole
Chinese	Russian
Dutch	Samy
Finnish	(Norwegian Laplanders)
French	Sotho
(Canadian & Parisian)	(South Africa)
German	Spanish
Greek	(Argentina, Chicano,
Haitian Creole	Chile, Puerto Rico,
Hebrew	Spain, & others)
Hindi	Swedish
Hungarian	Thai
Icelandic	Turkish
Italian	Vietnamese
Japanese	Zulu

American youths to report relatively many problems may be an interesting research topic in its own right.

SUMMARY

The YSR, its scales, and profile are products of research, and they can be used in many ways to expand our knowledge through research. Like practical applications, research should use multiple sources of data about young people's functioning. For youths who are cognitively capable of providing structured self-reports, these reports can be a key focus for research. Because the YSR is not confined to a single theoretical viewpoint, it can be applied to research involving many types of questions, theories, and other assessment procedures.

This chapter presented reasons for using raw scale scores rather than T scores for most statistical purposes and outlined ways of combining data from boys and girls in research with the YSR. It also addressed applications to research areas including epidemiology, diagnosis, taxonomy, etiology, outcomes, services, abuse, medical conditions, and cross-cultural comparisons.

Chapter 11
Assessment Materials
Related to the YSR

Self-reports are clearly an important source of assessment data, especially for individuals who are cognitively capable of reliably reporting their competencies and problems. However, the modest correlations between self-reports and reports by others (Achenbach et al., 1987) indicate that multiple sources of data are needed for comprehensive assessment. For the ages spanned by the YSR, the CBCL/4-18 obtains parents' reports and the TRF obtains teachers' reports in formats that facilitate comparisons among the three instruments. These three instruments have 89 similar problem items in common, but each instrument also has additional items geared to the type of informant for whom the instrument is designed.

The *Integrative Guide for the 1991 CBCL/4-18, YSR, and TRF Profiles* (Achenbach, 1991a) presents the procedures used to develop the eight 1991 syndrome scales common to these three instruments. The *Guide* describes a microcomputer program that is available for entering, scoring, and comparing data from all three instruments. Separate Manuals are available that present detailed information on the development and use of the CBCL (Achenbach, 1991b) and TRF (Achenbach, 1991c).

In the *Integrative Guide*, findings on associations between the YSR, CBCL, and TRF have been presented to facilitate the general coordination of cross-informant data in assessment for clinical and research purposes. Here, we will focus on the degree of association between YSR scores obtained from boys and girls, CBCL scores obtained from their fathers and mothers, and TRF scores obtained from their teachers. The correlations are between the corresponding scales of the different instruments, but the items of the corresponding scales are not necessarily identical. As detailed in Chapter 3, the scales for the cross-informant syndromes include some items that are specific to a particular instrument. In addition, the wording of counterpart items varies among the instruments to make them appropriate for the particular informants.

To enable us to compare data on precisely the same subjects for the different combinations of informants, Dr. Michael Sawyer has graciously permitted us to use his data from a general population sample participating in a longitudinal study in Adelaide, Australia (Sawyer, 1990). Because subjects were not screened out according to referral status, a few of the subjects had been referred for mental health services, but most had not. A particular strength of this sample is that it provides independent ratings by fathers, mothers, teachers, and youths on the same subjects. The subjects were 183 boys and 179 girls aged 11 to 16. Although the findings may not be precisely generalizable to the United States or other countries, the standard American versions of the YSR, CBCL, and TRF were used. Furthermore, the mean YSR total problem scores were very similar to those obtained in our national normative sample. Excluding the items *Allergy* and *Asthma*, the Adelaide mean problem scores were 37.8 for boys and 38.5 for girls, compared to the American normative mean scores of 37.3 for boys and 38.9 for girls (shown in Table 3-3). Considering that the standard deviations ranged from 19.1 to 25.3, these differences of about 1/2 point in mean scores are negligible.

Comparisons of scores on the 89 items common to the YSR, CBCL, and TRF showed that the Adelaide YSR problem scores were considerably higher than the Adelaide CBCL or TRF scores (all comparisons $p < .01$ by t test). Similar elevations of YSR scores over CBCL and TRF scores have been found in our normative samples, as well as in Puerto Rican, German, and Dutch samples (Achenbach, Bird, et al., 1990;

Köferl, 1988, Remschmidt & Walter, 1989; Verhulst et al., 1989). The tendency for adolescents to report more problems than their parents or teachers thus seems to be quite general in a variety of cultures studied to date. The actual magnitude of the YSR, CBCL, and TRF problem scores differs somewhat among the various cultures. Although the Adelaide YSR scores were remarkably similar to those of our normative sample, the Adelaide CBCL problem scores tended to be higher than the American CBCL problem scores. Higher Australian CBCL scores were also obtained in a systematic comparison of a Sydney, Australia sample with our 1976 general population sample from Washington, D.C., Maryland, and Virginia (Achenbach, Hensley et al., 1990).

Table 11-1 presents Pearson correlations of boys' and girls' YSR ratings with ratings by their fathers, mothers, and teachers. The mean rs averaged across the competence scales and across the problem scales did not differ much in relation to the sex of the youth or the sex of the parent. The mean rs for the competence scales were .48 for fathers' ratings of their sons and .44 for ratings of their daughters. The corresponding rs for mothers' ratings were .55 for their sons and .57 for their daughters. For the problem scales, the mean rs were .56 for fathers' ratings of their sons, .49 for fathers' ratings of their daughters, .59 for mothers' ratings of their sons, and .52 for mothers' ratings of their daughters.

Teachers' ratings yielded rs of .51 with boys' versus .55 with girls' YSR ratings of academic performance and mean rs of .48 for boys' problem scores versus .35 for girls' problem scores. The tendency for teachers' ratings to agree better with YSR problem ratings by boys than by girls did not reach statistical significance ($p = .065$). However, it was consistent with findings of higher correlations for boys than girls between TRF and YSR problem ratings, as well as between TRF and CBCL ratings, in larger samples (Achenbach, 1991a).

Of the eight syndromes common to the three instruments, the rs for the Social Problems syndrome were consistently

Table 11-1

Correlations of YSR Ratings with CBCL and TRF Ratings

Scale	183ᵃ Boys x			179ᵃ Girls x			Mean r
	Fathers	Mothers	Teachers	Fathers	Mothers	Teachers	
Activities	.36	.68	—	.46	.46	—	.50
Social	.55	.47	—	.32	.58	—	.49
Academic Performance	.61	.58	.51	.34	.54	.55	.53
Total Competence	.39	.42	—	.60	.67	—	.53
Mean r	.48	.55	—	.44	.57	—	.51
Withdrawn	.48	.47	.50	.42	.43	.36	.44
Somatic Complaints	.29	.37	(.15)	.46	.43	.20	.32
Anxious/Depressed	.54	.53	.46	.46	.51	.26	.46
Social Problems	.68	.67	.60	.60	.63	.55	.62
Thought Problems	.22	.31	.30	.31	.26	.20	.27
Attention Problems	.65	.66	.53	.52	.59	.41	.57
Delinquent Behavior	.67	.71	.55	.51	.52	.45	.58
Aggressive Behavior	.62	.65	.52	.46	.57	.33	.53
Internalizing	.53	.51	.51	.51	.56	.31	.49
Externalizing	.68	.71	.55	.52	.59	.39	.58
Total Problems	.67	.69	.55	.55	.59	.38	.58
Mean r	.56	.59	.48	.49	.52	.35	.50

Note. All rs were significant at p <.03 except the one in parentheses. Mean rs were computed by z transformations. Data were from an Australian general population sample participating in a longitudinal study by Sawyer (1990).
ᵃNs for competence scores ranged from 62-67 because the competence portion of the YSR was optional.

among the highest for all combinations of raters and yielded the highest mean r across all combinations. Where self-reports by adolescents are concerned, the Social Problems syndrome may thus tap an area of particular consistency among informants' perceptions.

The mean rs shown in Table 11-1 were considerably higher than the mean r of .25 between self- and parent-reports and .20 between self- and teacher-reports obtained in our meta-analyses of many studies using different instruments (Achenbach et al., 1987). The lower correlations obtained in the meta-analyses might be partly accounted for by the wider age range included there. That is, parents and teachers might agree less with both younger and older youths than with the 11- to 16-year-olds in Sawyer's (1990) sample. Higher inter-informant correlations than in our meta-analyses have also been obtained when the YSR was used in our normative sample, as well as in Puerto Rican and Dutch samples (Achenbach, 1991a; Achenbach, Bird et al., 1990; Verhulst & van der Ende, 1991).

YOUNG ADULT SELF-REPORT

Because self-reports become increasingly important as youths grow older, we have developed a counterpart of the YSR designed for ages 19 to 27. Called the Young Adult Self-Report (YASR; Achenbach, 1990b), it has counterparts of many YSR items, plus additional items concerning work, higher education, marital and similar relationships, alcohol, and drug use. A form to be completed by parents, called the Young Adult Behavior Checklist (YABCL; Achenbach, 1990a) has also been developed to obtain parental perspectives on young adults' behavior analogous to the parental perspectives obtained with the CBCL. As research on these instruments progresses, scoring profiles will be made available, along with reliability and validity data.

SUMMARY

This chapter presented correlations between corresponding scales of the YSR, CBCL, and TRF, separately for boys and girls. The magnitude of the correlations between YSR and CBCL ratings did not differ much for boys versus girls or mothers versus fathers. Correlations between YSR and TRF problem ratings tended to be somewhat higher for boys than for girls. The cross-informant correlations were considerably higher than the correlations obtained with self-reports obtained in meta-analyses of studies using many different instruments. Agreement among the YSR, CBCL, and TRF was especially good on the Social Problems syndrome, where the mean r was .62 across all combinations of raters.

To extend empirically based assessment into young adulthood, the Young Adult Self-Report (YASR) has been developed to obtain self-reports in a format like that of the YSR. The Young Adult Behavior Checklist (YABCL) has been developed to obtain reports by parents of young adults.

Chapter 12
Answers to Commonly
Asked Questions

The purpose of this chapter is to answer questions that may arise about the YSR and profile. Although earlier sections of the *Manual* address many of these questions, we list them here to provide explicit answers, supplemented by references to more detailed information where relevant. The questions are grouped according to whether they refer mainly to the content of the YSR, scoring the YSR, or the YSR profile. If you have a question that is not found under one heading, look under the other headings as well. The Table of Contents and Index may also help you find answers to questions not listed here. For questions about relations between the YSR and the 1991 CBCL/4-18 and TRF consult the *Integrative Guide for the 1991 CBCL/4-18, YSR, and TRF Profiles* (Achenbach, 1991a).

QUESTIONS ABOUT THE YSR

1. How does the 1991 YSR differ from previous editions of the YSR?

Answer: Small changes have been made to clarify the wording of a few items, such as the following: *Competence Item V.2* (page 2)—the word *any* has been inserted before the word *friends* to indicate that not only the "close friends" indicated in item V.1 are to be included in the frequency of contacts with friends. *Problem Item 42* (page 3)—the wording has been changed to *I would rather be alone than with others*, from *I like to be alone. Problem Item 56a* (page 3)—(*not headaches*) has been added to clarify that headaches should not be included with "aches or pains." These changes do not affect scoring. The 1991 YSR can be scored on the pre-1991 profile. Conversely, the 1991 YSR can be scored on the 1991 profile.

2. Why is the YSR said to have 102 specific problem items and 16 socially desirable items, when the item numbers only go to 112?

Answer: Item *56* includes seven specific physical complaints designated as *a* through *g*. Combined with the remaining 95 specifically stated problems, this sums to 102 problem items. In addition, Item *56h* provides space for respondents to enter any physical problems not otherwise listed. Items *2. Allergy* and *4. Asthma* are no longer included in the total problem score, because they did not discriminate significantly between referred and nonreferred samples on the YSR or CBCL/4-18. Total problem scores are computed as the sum of 1s and 2s for the remaining 100 specific problem items + item *56h*. If a 2 is scored for all 100 items and *56h*, the total score would be 202.

3. What is done with the 16 socially desirable items?

Answer: These items were inserted to replace CBCL problem items that were deemed inappropriate to ask adolescents. To mitigate the list of problem items, they refer to socially desirable characteristics that most youths can endorse about themselves. Most youths do, in fact, endorse them, but nonreferred youths scored themselves significantly higher than referred youths on some of these items.

4. Why doesn't the YSR have items for special class placement, grade repetition, and school problems like those on the CBCL?

Answer: These items were omitted from the YSR, because they were deemed to be potentially embarrassing to youths and less accurately reported by youths than by their parents or teachers. Page 2 of the YSR does provide space for the youth to "describe any concerns or problems you have about school." The responses entered here are clinically useful, but they are not scored on the YSR profile.

5. What if a youth's reading skills are poor?

Answer: If a youth's reading skills are below the 5th grade reading level, the YSR should be read aloud by an interviewer who records the youth's answers. If the youth's reading skills are questionable, one copy of the YSR can be handed to the youth while the interviewer retains a second copy. The interviewer then says: "I'm going to read the questions on this form and I'll write down your answers." Most youths who can read adequately will soon start answering the questions before they are read, but this procedure avoids embarrassment for those who cannot read well. If the YSR is administered orally, it should be done in a private location, out of earshot of others.

6. What if a youth can't read English but can read another language?

Answer: At this writing, we know of translations of the CBCL into the 33 languages listed in Table 10-3. Contact Dr. Achenbach for the current status of YSR translations.

7. Can social desirability, lying, and other informant characteristics cause biases in YSR scores?

Answer: Informant characteristics may be associated with scores on all kinds of questionnaires, including the YSR. Because any reports by any informants may be affected by characteristics of the informants, no single informant's reports can provide a complete picture. It is the user's task to construct a comprehensive picture of the youth from multiple sources and types of data. Questions 7 and 12 in the section on the profile provide guidelines for evaluating scores that are so low or high as to suggest gross distortions or errors. Chapter 5 of this Manual provides data on reliability, while the cross-informant computer program displays comparisons and correlations between informants' reports for a particular child.

8. Can the YSR be used for ages below 11 and over 18?

Answer: We did not norm the YSR below the age of 11, because too large a proportion of younger children— especially those referred for mental health services—would have inadequate cognitive or reading skills. We did not norm the YSR above the age of 18, because many of the items are less relevant beyond that age and it is difficult to obtain representative general population samples during the period of transition between the family of origin and young adults' establishment of their own households. Although the YSR can be used with bright 9- and 10-year-olds and with some 19- and 20-year-olds, the user should be aware that the norms are not directly applicable to these ages. For respondents outside the target age range, the focus should therefore be on the specific content of responses, comparisons between the same respondents' raw scores on different occasions, and comparisons between respondents of the same age. We have developed the *Semistructured Clinical Interview for Children (SCIC)* (McConaughy & Achenbach, 1990) for direct assessment of 6-11-year-olds. We have also developed an upward extension of the YSR called the *Young Adult Self-Report (YASR)*. Contact Dr. Achenbach about scales for scoring the YASR.

9. Can the YSR be used with physically or mentally handicapped youths?

Answer: The norms for the YSR are based on representative general population samples of youths free of major handicaps. If handicapped youths are capable of responding to the YSR either by filling it out themselves or by responding orally, their responses are valuable for identifying specific areas of concern, for assessing change from one occasion to another, and for comparison with normative samples of nonhandicapped youths. This may be especially useful for evaluating handicapped youths who must mix with nonhandicapped people, as in mainstream situations. Even though a handicap is known to contribute to particular problems, it is still important to know the specific forms and degrees of deviance indicated by the youth's self-report. However, a mental age of at least 10 years is needed to ensure adequate comprehension of the items.

10. Page 3 of the YSR instructs the respondent to base ratings on the previous 6 months. What if the user wants the respondent to focus on a shorter period or wants to readminister the YSR over intervals of less than 6 months?

Answer: The 6-month instruction can be changed to suit the interval desired. If the interval is reduced much below 6 months, this may reduce scores on some items and scales. Low frequency problems, such as suicide attempts and firesetting, may also be missed if the rating interval is too short. If reassessments are planned for intervals of less than 6 months, however, the instructions should be changed to use the same shortened interval for each rating. If follow-up ratings are to be done after a 3-month interval, for example, the respondent should be instructed to base both the initial and follow-up ratings on 3-month periods. Otherwise, scores may be higher at one rating merely because a longer rating period was specified than for the other rating. Although brief intervals are not recommended for raters such as parents because time is required for them to become aware of changes in behavior, intervals as short as a few days or a week may be acceptable for YSR self-ratings to monitor responses to specific interventions. It should be remembered, however, that the shorter the interval on which ratings are based, the more vulnerable the results are to random and transient changes.

11. Is there a short form of the YSR that takes less time to fill out?

Answer: There is not a short form as such. However, the competence portion of the YSR (pages 1 and 2) or problem portion (pages 3 and 4) can be administered alone. Because each of these is brief and each scale's scores require that all the constituent items of the scale are considered by the respondent, it would not make sense to abbreviate the YSR any farther.

12. Is there a machine-readable form of the YSR?

Answer: We have developed a machine-readable YSR that can be processed by fax boards and scanners. To employ the machine-readable YSR, you need either a reflective-read scanner, such as those produced by NCS, Scantron, and Scanning Dynamics, or Teleform software for use with image scanners and fax boards. You also need an IBM-compatible computer with software that is appropriate for your scanner, plus our Scanning Software Package to convert data from the machine-readable YSR to input for the YSR or Cross-Informant scoring program. For details, send inquiries to the fax number or address shown on page ii of this Manual.

SCORING THE YSR

Appendix A provides detailed scoring instructions, including criteria for items the respondent is asked to describe.

1. What if the respondent scores two items when his/her comments indicate that they both refer to exactly the same problem?

Answer: Score only the item that most specifically describes the problem. For example, suppose a respondent circled 2 for Item *9. I can't get my mind off certain thoughts (describe)* and wrote in "sex." And the respondent also circled 2 for Item *96. I think about sex too much.* Because Item *96* covers the problem more specifically than Item *9*, only the 2 for Item *96* should be counted, whereas Item *9* should be rescored as 0.

2. What if a boy writes in "girls" for Item *9. I can't get my mind off certain thoughts (describe)?*

Answer: On the CBCL and TRF, Item *9* includes the word *obsessions* and is scored to exclude problems that are clearly not obsessional. Because youths may not be familiar with the term "obsession," it is not included in the YSR item. Furthermore, youths' reports of preoccupying thoughts are apt to be important even if they do not qualify as obsessions. The scoring of Item *9* is therefore not as restrictive on the YSR as on the CBCL and TRF. Except for responses that are more specifically covered by other items, as illustrated in #1 above, YSR Item *9* should be scored as the youth scored it. Thus, even though it might be quite normal for a boy to be preoccupied with girls, the score entered by the youth should be left intact. (Note that, if the respondent had written "sex" for Item *9*, Item *96* should be scored instead, as described in #1 above.)

3. What if a respondent writes "ringing in ears" for Item *40. I hear sounds or voices that other people think aren't there (describe)* or writes "spots before eyes" for Item *70. I see things that other people think aren't there (describe)?*

Answer: As with Item *9*, these items should be scored as the respondent scored them, unless the descriptions indicate that they are more specifically covered by another item. Because youths may interpret these items in various ways, they do not necessarily indicate hallucinations. It is only when these items, plus other items on the Thought Problems scale, sum to a deviant scale score that clinical deviance is indicated. Whenever these items are scored as present, the youth's comments on the YSR and follow-up interviews should be used to determine their basis.

4. What if the respondent circles two scores for a particular item or otherwise indicates that the item is true but does not clearly indicate a score of 1 or 2?

Answer: Score the item 1.

5. How is Item *56h* figured in the total score?

Answer: If the respondent has entered for Item *56h* a physical problem without known medical cause that is not specifically covered by an item listed on the YSR, add the 1 or 2 scored by the respondent for *56h* to the 1s and 2s for all other problem items. If the respondent has entered more than one additional physical problem, count only the one having the highest score. Thus, if a respondent gave one additional physical problem a score of 1 and another additional physical problem a score of 2, add 2 to the total problem score. (Adding a maximum of 2 points for Item *56h* is intended to limit the amount of variance contributed by items that are not stated for other respondents to rate.)

6. What is done with responses to the open-ended items regarding illnesses, school concerns, other concerns, and best things on page 2 and "anything else that describes your feelings, behavior, or interests" on page 4?

Answer: The entries in these spaces are often clinically useful and helpful as a basis for interviewing youths, but they are not scored.

7. Should YSRs that have many unanswered items be scored?

Answer: The scoring instructions (Appendix A) give rules for dealing with unanswered items. In brief, if one item is omitted from the Social scale, the mean of the other items of that scale is substituted for the missing item. If more than one item is missing from the Social scale, do *not* score the scale. Do *not* score the Activities scale if any of the four items is missing. Do *not* score Academic Performance if the respondent checked boxes for *fewer than 3* academic subjects. Do *not* compute the total competence score unless scores are available for Activities, Social, and Academic Performance. On the problem portion of the YSR, do *not* compute scale scores or the total problem score if *more than 8* problem items were left blank (not counting Items *2, 4,* and *56h*), unless it is clear that the respondent intended the blanks to be zeroes.

8. How are the total competence and problem scores used?

Answer: These scores provide global indices of self-reported competencies and problems. We have found that the competence *T* scores of 40 and the problem *T* scores of 60 provide good cutpoints for discrimination between clinically referred and nonreferred youths (see Chapter 6 for details of the cutpoints). The total problem score can also be used as a basis for comparing problems in different groups and for assessing change as a function of time or intervention. The total competence score can be used in similar ways, but it is not as strong a discriminator between referred and nonreferred youths.

THE YSR PROFILE

1. How does the 1991 profile differ from the previous edition?

Answer: Chapters 2 and 3 describe the 1991 profile scales in detail. Briefly, the main innovations include: (*a*) scoring youths in terms of the same eight syndromes and the same Internalizing and Externalizing groupings for both sexes on the YSR and all sex/age groups on the CBCL/4-18 and TRF; (*b*) use of a new national sample to norm the profiles of all three instruments; (*c*) extension of syndrome *T* scores down to 50; (*d*) demarcation of a borderline clinical range; and (*e*) easier computation of Internalizing and Externalizing scores on the hand-scored profile.

2. Can hand scoring be made quicker and easier?

Answer: We offer scoring templates that fit over the YSR to indicate the scales on which the problem items are scored. The 1991 YSR profile is easier than the previous edition to score by hand, because the same templates are used for both sexes. Furthermore, to compute the Internalizing and Externalizing scores, the individual items no longer need to be entered and scored. The time taken to score profiles usually decreases with experience. However, we recommend computer scoring whenever feasible, as this is quicker, more accurate, and stores scores for subsequent analysis, as well as printing hard-copy profiles whenever desired.

3. Why are some problems included on more than one profile scale?

Answer: As explained in Chapter 3, problem items are included on each syndrome for which they met criteria for the cross-informant syndrome constructs. In addition, a few items that met criteria for the YSR core syndromes are included in the YSR versions of the syndrome scales. Item *103. Unhappy, sad, or depressed,* is included on two Internalizing scales, but it is counted only once toward the Internalizing score. No item of the Externalizing scales is included on more than one of the eight cross-informant syndrome scales.

4. Why are there no norms for the "Other Problems" listed on the profile?

Answer: The "Other Problems" on the profile do *not* constitute a scale. They are merely problems that were either reported too seldom to be included in the derivation of syndromes or did not qualify for the syndrome scales. There are thus no associations among them to warrant treating them as a scale. However, each of these problems may be important in its own right, and they are included in the total problem score.

5. Should raw scores or *T* scores be used to report results?

Answer: Chapter 10 discusses the different uses of raw scores and *T* scores in detail.

6. Does a high score on the Delinquent Behavior scale mean that a youth is a juvenile delinquent?

Answer: The names of the scales are mainly intended to summarize the content of the scales. The term "Delinquent Behavior" literally refers to "conduct that is out of accord with accepted behavior or law" and "offending by neglect or violation of duty or law" (Mish, 1988, p. 336). Although some items of the Delinquent Behavior syndrome, such as stealing, are illegal, a high score on the scale for this syndrome does not necessarily mean that a youth has broken laws or will be adjudicated as a delinquent. Instead, it means that the youth is reported to engage in more behaviors of the empirically derived Delinquent Behavior syndrome than are reported for normative samples of peers. Similarly, the labels for other syndromes provide summary descriptions for the kinds of problems included in the syndromes, rather than being directly equivalent to any administrative or diagnostic category.

7. Should extremely low scores on any problem scales be considered deviant?

Answer: Low scores merely reflect the absence of reported problems. As explained in Chapter 3, the profile compresses the low end of the syndrome scales, so that 50 is the minimum T score obtainable on these scales. If a user wishes to retain all the differentiation possible at the low end of these scales, raw scores can be employed. However, it should be remembered that all the scores assigned a T score of 50 are well within the normal range. They should not, therefore, be construed as indicating different degrees of deviance. Extremely low total problem scores may suggest that the respondent has not understood the YSR or has not been candid, as discussed in answer to Question 12.

8. Should there be separate norms for different socioeconomic or ethnic groups?

Answer: Chapter 6 shows that socioeconomic and ethnic differences are generally too small to warrant separate norms.

9. How can comparisons be made between profile scores for boys and girls?

Answer: Except for the Self-Destructive/Identity Problems syndrome that was found only for boys, all the 1991 YSR scales are the same for both sexes. However, to reflect sex differences in prevalence rates, the scales are normed separately for each sex. To include YSR scores for boys and girls in the same analyses, use the T scores computed from the scales for each sex. When data from both sexes are combined in the same analysis, however, it is always advisable to retain sex as a dimension of the analysis, both to take account of sex differences in the distribution of scores and to identify any interactions between sex and other variables.

11. How are interpretations of the profile made?

Answer: The YSR profile is intended as a standardized summary of the competencies and problems reported by a youth and compared to those reported by other youths of the same sex. As such, it is to be compared and integrated with everything else that is known about the youth, instead of being "interpreted" in isolation.   Additional relevant data include other people's descriptions of the youth—such as parents' reports on the CBCL, teachers' reports on the TRF, and observers' reports on the DOF; developmental history; tests of cognitive ability, academic achievement, and perceptual-motor functioning;   biomedical data;   and clinical interviews and observations. Guidelines and case illustrations are provided in Chapter 9.

12. Is there a "lie" scale for the profile?

Answer: Deliberate lying is only one type of bias that can lead to excessively low or high scores, depending on whether the respondent denies or exaggerates problems.   Social desirability sets, overscrupulousness, and misunderstandings can also affect ratings.   In view of the variety of possible biases, we did not add items intended to detect every possible type of bias. Instead, we stress that profile scores should never be used to make decisions in isolation from other information about the respondent. The scores should always be compared with other data to identify major discrepancies or distortions and to determine the reasons. Extremely low or high scores for competence or problems should always be followed up to determine whether they accurately reflect the respondents' views of themselves. If they accurately reflect the respondents' views, do these views differ markedly from the views of others, such as parents, teachers, and practitioners?

Because most youths report a substantial number of problems, extremely low scores are so uncommon as to suggest that the respondent has not understood the YSR or is not being candid. The mean total problem scores in our normative samples were 37.3 for boys and 38.9 for girls. Total problem scores of 0-6 were obtained by only 2% of our normative samples and should therefore be followed up to determine whether they accurately reflect the respondents' views. Scores from 7 to 10 for boys and 7 to 8 for girls are low enough to hint at a tendency to deny problems, but might accurately reflect the respondents' views.

Based on the distributions of total problem scores in our clinical samples, scores above 147 for boys and 141 for girls are so *high* as to raise questions about exaggeration or misunderstanding.

13. Why is there no School scale on the YSR profile?

Answer: As discussed in Chapters 1 and 2, we did not deem it appropriate to have youths report special class placement, repeating grades, and school problems as parents report them on the CBCL. Because the only school item scorable on the competence portion of the YSR is the youth's self-ratings for performance in academic subjects, this is an insufficient basis for a separate scale. However, the mean of the youth's self-ratings for academic performance is included in the total competence score.

REFERENCES

Abramowitz, M. & Stegun, I.A. (1968). *Handbook of mathematical functions*. Washington, D.C.: National Bureau of Standards.

Achenbach, T.M. (1966). The classification of children's psychiatric symptoms: A factor-analytic study. *Psychological Monographs, 80* (No. 615).

Achenbach, T.M. (1990a). *Young Adult Behavior Checklist*. Burlington, VT: University of Vermont Department of Psychiatry.

Achenbach, T.M. (1990b). *Young Adult Self-Report*. Burlington, VT: University of Vermont Department of Psychiatry.

Achenbach, T.M. (1991a). *Integrative Guide for the 1991 CBCL/4-18, YSR, and TRF Profiles*. Burlington, VT: University of Vermont Department of Psychiatry.

Achenbach, T.M. (1991b). *Manual for the Child Behavior Checklist/4-18 and 1991 Profile*. Burlington, VT: University of Vermont Department of Psychiatry.

Achenbach, T.M. (1991c). *Manual for the Teacher's Report Form and 1991 Profile*. Burlington, VT: University of Vermont Department of Psychiatry.

Achenbach, T.M., Bird, H.R., Canino, G.J., Phares, V., Gould, M., & Rubio-Stipec, M. (1990). Epidemiological comparisons of Puerto Rican and U.S. mainland children: Parent, teacher, and self reports. *Journal of the American Academy of Child and Adolescent Psychiatry, 29*, 84-93.

Achenbach, T.M., & Brown, J.S. (1991). *Bibliography of published studies using the Child Behavior Checklist and related materials: 1991 edition*. Burlington, VT: University of Vermont Department of Psychiatry.

Achenbach, T.M., & Edelbrock, C. (1978). The classification of child psychopathology: A review and analysis of empirical efforts. *Psychological Bulletin, 85*, 1275-1301.

Achenbach, T.M., & Edelbrock, C. (1981). Behavioral problems and competencies reported by parents of normal and disturbed children aged four to sixteen. *Monographs of the Society for Research in Child Development, 46* (Serial No. 188).

Achenbach, T.M., & Edelbrock, C. (1983). *Manual for the Child Behavior Checklist and Revised Child Behavior Profile*. Burlington, VT: University of Vermont Department of Psychiatry.

Achenbach, T.M., & Edelbrock, C. (1986). *Manual for the Teacher's Report Form and Teacher Version of the Child Behavior Profile*. Burlington, VT: University of Vermont Department of Psychiatry.

Achenbach, T.M. & Edelbrock, C. (1987). *Manual for the Youth Self-Report and Profile*. Burlington, VT: University of Vermont Department of Psychiatry.

Achenbach, T.M., Hensley, V.R., Phares, V.S., & Grayson, D. (1990). Problems and competencies reported by parents of Australian and American children. *Journal of Child Psychology and Psychiatry, 31*, 265-286.

Achenbach, T.M., & Lewis, M. (1971). A proposed model for clinical research and its application to encopresis and enuresis. *Journal of the American Academy of Child Psychiatry, 10*, 535-554.

Achenbach, T.M. & McConaughy, S.H. (1987). *Empirically based assessment of child and adolescent psychopathology: Practical applications*. Newbury Park, CA: Sage.

American Psychiatric Association (1952, 1968, 1980, 1987). *Diagnostic and statistical manual of mental disorders* (1st ed., 2nd ed., 3rd ed., 3rd ed. rev.). Washington, D.C.: Author.

Bernstein, G.A., & Garfinkel, D.B. (1986). School phobia: The overlap of affective and anxiety disorders. *Journal of the American Academy of Child Psychiatry, 25*, 235-241.

Cohen, J. (1988). *Statistical power analysis for the behavioral sciences* (2nd ed.). New York: Academic Press.

Cole, D.A. (1987). Methodological contributions to clinical research: Utility of confirmatory factor analysis in test validation research. *Journal of Consulting and Clinical Psychology, 55*, 584-594.

Crocker, L., & Algina, J. (1986). *Introduction to classical and modern test theory*. New York: Holt, Rinehart, & Winston.

Cronbach, L.J. (1951). Coefficient alpha and the internal structure of tests. *Psychometrika, 16*, 297-334.

Edelbrock, C., & Costello, A.J. (1988). Convergence between statistically derived behavior problem syndromes and child psychiatric diagnoses. *Journal of Abnormal Child Psychology, 16*, 219-231.

Edelbrock, C., Costello, A.J., Dulcan, M.K., Kalas, R., & Conover, N.C. (1985). Age differences in the reliability of the psychiatric interview of the child. *Child Development, 56*, 265-275.

Edelbrock, C., Costello, A.J., & Kessler, M.D. (1984). Empirical corroboration of attention deficit disorder. *Journal of the American Academy of Child Psychiatry, 23*, 285-290.

Edelbrock, C., Greenbaum, R., & Conover, N.C. (1985). Reliability and concurrent relations between the Teacher Version of the Child Behavior Profile and the Conners Revised Teacher Rating Scale. *Journal of Abnormal Child Psychology, 13*, 295-304.

Education of the Handicapped Act. (1977). *Federal Register, 42*, p. 42478. Amended in *Federal Register*, (1981), *46*, p. 3866.

Evans, W.R. (1975). The Behavior Problem Checklist. Data from an inner city population. *Psychology in the Schools, 12*, 301-303.

Fleiss, J.L. (1981). *Statistical methods for rates and proportions* (2nd ed.). New York: Wiley.

Gorsuch, R.L. (1983). *Factor analysis* (2nd ed.). Hillsdale, NJ: Erlbaum.

Guilford, J.P. (1965). *Fundamental statistics in psychology and education* (4th ed.). New York: McGraw-Hill.

Harter, S. (1982). The Perceived Competence Scale for Children. *Child Development, 53*, 87-97.

Hollingshead, A.B. (1975). *Four factor index of social status*. Unpublished paper. New Haven, CT: Yale University, Department of Sociology.

Katz, P.A., Zigler, E., & Zalk, S.R. (1975). Children's self-image disparity: The effects of age, maladjustment and action-thought orientation. *Developmental Psychology, 11*, 546-550.

Kazdin, A.E., French, N.H., & Unis, A.S. (1983). Child, mother, and father evaluations of depression in psychiatric inpatient children. *Journal of Abnormal Child Psychology, 11*, 167-180.

Köferl, P. (1988). *Invulnerabilität und Stressresistenz: Theoretische und empirische Befund zur effectiven Bewältigen von psychosozialen Stressoren*. Inaugural-Dissertation, University of Bielefeld, Germany.

McConaughy, S.H., & Achenbach, T.M. (1990). *Guide for the Semistructured Clinical Interview for Children Aged 6-11*. Burlington, VT: University of Vermont Department of Psychiatry.

McConaughy, S.H., Achenbach, T.M., & Gent, C.L. (1988). Multiaxial empirically based assessment: Parent, teacher, observational, cognitive, and personality correlates of Child Behavior Profiles for 6-11-year-old boys. *Journal of Abnormal Child Psychology, 16*, 485-509.

McConaughy, S.H., Stanger, C., & Achenbach, T.M. (1991). Three-year prediction of behavioral/emotional problems and signs of disturbance in a national sample of 4- to 16-year-olds: I. Categorical versus quantitative predictive relations. Submitted for publication.

Milich, R., Roberts, M., Loney, J., & Caputo, J. (1980). Differentiating practice effects and statistical regression on the Conners Hyperkinesis Index. *Journal of Abnormal Child Psychology, 8*, 549-552.

Miller, L.C. (1967). Louisville Behavior Checklist for males, 6-12 years of age. *Psychological Reports, 21*, 885-896.

Miller, L.C., Hampe, E., Barrett, C.L., & Noble, H. (1972). Test-retest reliability of parent ratings of children's deviant behavior. *Psychological Reports, 31*, 249-250.

Mish, F.C. (Ed.). (1988). *Webster's ninth new collegiate dictionary.* Springfield, MA: Merriam-Webster.

Peterson, D.R. (1961). Behavior problems of middle childhood. *Journal of Consulting Psychology, 25*, 205-209.

Piers, E.V. (1972). Parent predictions of children's self-concepts. *Journal of Consulting and Clinical Psychology, 38*, 428-433.

Remschmidt, H., & Walter, R. (1990). *Psychische Auffälligkeiten bei Schulkindern.* Göttingen: Verlag für Psychologie.

Robins, L.N. (1985). Epidemiology: Reflections on testing the validity of psychiatric interviews. *Archives of General Psychiatry, 42*, 918-924.

Sakoda, J.M., Cohen, B.H., & Beall, G. (1954). Test of significance for a series of statistical tests. *Psychological Bulletin, 51*, 172-175.

SAS Institute, (1988). *SAS/STAT User's Guide, Release 6.03 Edition.* Cary, NC: SAS Institute.

Sawyer, M.G. (1990). Childhood behavior problems: Discrepancies between reports from children, parents, and teachers. Unpublished Ph.D. dissertation. University of Adelaide, Australia.

Saylor, C.F., Finch, A.J., Spirito, A., & Bennett, B. (1984). The children's depression inventory: A systematic evaluation of psychometric properties. *Journal of Consulting and Clinical Psychology, 52*, 955-967.

Snook, S.C., & Gorsuch, R.L. (1989). Component analysis versus common factor analysis: A Monte Carlo study. *Psychological Bulletin, 106*, 148-154.

Strauss, C.C., Last, C.G., Hersen, M., & Kazdin, A.E. (1988). Association between anxiety and depression in children and adolescents with anxiety disorders. *Journal of Abnormal Child Psychology, 16*, 57-68.

Swets, J.E., & Pickett, R.M. (1982). *Evaluation of diagnostic systems: Methods from signal detection theory.* New York: Academic Press.

Treiber, F.A. & Mabe, P.A. (1987). Child and parent perceptions of children's psychopathology in psychiatric outpatient children. *Journal of Abnormal Child Psychology, 15*, 115-124.

Verhulst, F.C., Prince, J., Vervuurt-Poot, C., & de Jong, J.B. (1989). Mental health in Dutch children: (IV) Self-reported problems for ages 11-18. *Acta Psychiatrica Scandinavica, 80* (Suppl. 356).

Verhulst, F.C., & van der Ende, J. (1991). Agreement between parents' reports and adolescents' self-reports of problem behavior. Submitted for publication.

Wechsler, D. (1989). *Wechsler Preschool and Primary Scale of Intelligence-Revised*. San Antonio: Psychological Corporation.

Weinstein, S.R., Noam, G.G., Grimes, K., Stone, K., & Schwab-Stone, M. (1990). Convergence of DSM-III diagnoses and self-reported symptoms in child and adolescent inpatients. *Journal of the American Academy of Child and Adolescent Psychiatry, 29*, 627-634.

Weintraub, S.A. (1973). Self-control as a correlate of an internalizing-externalizing symptom dimension. *Journal of Abnormal Child Psychology, 1*, 292-307.

Zimet, S.G. & Farley, G.K. (1986). Four perspectives on the competence and self-esteem of emotionally disturbed children beginning day treatment. *Journal of the American Academy of Child Psychiatry, 25*, 76-83.

Zimet, S.G. & Farley, G.K. (1987). How do emotionally disturbed children report their competencies and self-worth? *Journal of the American Academy of Child and Adolescent Psychiatry, 26*, 33-38.

APPENDIX A
INSTRUCTIONS FOR HAND SCORING
THE YOUTH SELF-REPORT

Note. There are small differences between the hand-scored and computer-scored data entry formats, but they produce the same results. Templates are available to assist in transferring data from pp. 3-4 of the YSR to the profile. Be sure to use the column of scale scores appropriate for the sex of the respondent.

Scoring the Competence Items

The following two items are *not* scored on the competence scales, but their scores can be entered in the box provided to the right of profile:

I-A. # of sports.   If youth reported 0 or 1 sport — enter 0 in box
2 sports — enter 1 in box
3 or more sports — enter 2 in box

II-A. # of other activities. If youth reported 0 or 1 activity — enter 0 in box
2 activities — enter 1 in box
3 or more activities — enter 2 in box
Do not count listening to radio or TV, goofing off, or the like as activities.

ACTIVITIES SCALE—Do *not* score if data are missing for any of the 4 scores comprising the scale. The Roman numerals correspond to those on pages 1 and 2 of the YSR and on the profile scoring form. If a youth checked more than 1 box where only 1 should be checked, score the box closest to "average."

I-B. Mean of participation & skill in sports. If youth reported no sports, enter 0.
For each response of *less than average* or *below average* — score 0
average — score 1
more than average or *above average* — score 2
Excluding blanks and "don't know" responses, compute the *mean* of these scores by summing them and dividing by the number of scores you have summed. Enter this mean on the profile.

II-B. Mean of participation & skill in activities. Compute in the same way as specified in I-B for sports.

IV-A. # of jobs.   If youth reported 0 or 1 job — enter 0 on profile
2 jobs — enter 1 on profile
3 or more jobs — enter 2 on profile

IV-B. Mean job quality. Compute as specified in I-B.

Total score for Activities Scale. Sum the 4 scores just entered. Round off total to nearest .5.

210

SOCIAL SCALE—Do *not* score if data are missing for more than 1 of the 6 scores.

III-A. # of organizations. If youth checked 0 or 1 — enter 0 on profile
2 — enter 1 on profile
3 or more — enter 2 on profile

III-B. Mean of participation in organizations. Compute as specified in I-B.

V-1. # of friends. If youth checked *0 or 1* — enter 0 on profile
2 or 3 — enter 1 on profile
4 or more — enter 2 on profile

V-2. Contacts with friends. If youth checked *less than 1* — enter 0 on profile
On the 1991 profile, this item can be scored   *1 or 2* — enter 1 on profile
1 or 2 even if no close friends were reported   *3 or more* — enter 2 on profile
in Item V-I.

VI-A. Behavior with others. For each of the first three items (Items a, b, & c):
If the youth checked *worse* — score 0
about average — score 1
better — score 2
Excluding any items for which the youth did not check a box, compute the
mean of these scores and enter it on the profile.

VI-B. Do things by self.   If the youth checked *worse*— enter 0 on profile
(Item d)   *about average*— enter 1 on profile
better— enter 2 on profile

Total score for Social Scale. Sum the 6 scores just entered for the items of the
Social scale. If missing data prevent computation of 1 score, substitute the *mean*
of the other 5 scores for the missing score in computing the total. Round off total
to nearest .5.

ACADEMIC PERFORMANCE — This does not constitute a profile scale, but
is added to scores for Activities and Social to obtain a total competence score.
Do *not* score if youth has checked boxes for *less than 3* academic subjects.

VII-1. Mean performance. For each academic subject checked:
failing — score 0
below average — score 1
average — score 2
above average — score 3
Compute the *mean* of these scores, rounded to the nearest .5. (Academic
subjects include reading, writing, arithmetic, spelling, science, English, foreign
language, history, social studies, computer programming, and similar subjects.

Do *not* count physical education, art, music, home economics, driver education, industrial arts, typing, or the like.)

Note. Comments written by youth in the spaces below Item VII are *not* scored.

TOTAL COMPETENCE SCORE. Sum the total raw scores for Activities, Social, and Academic Performance. Do *not* compute a total competence score unless scores are available for all 3 of these. *T* scores for total competence scores are in the box to the right of the profile. Mark the youth's total competence raw score under the appropriate heading of the box. After you have found the youth's raw score, look to the right for the *T* score. *Be sure to mark the number in the column appropriate for the youth's sex.*

Scoring the Problem Scales

Do *not* score if data are missing for more than 8 problem items, not counting Items 2, 4, or 56h. If a youth circled two numbers for an item, score the item 1. Note that there are 103 problem items, even though the numbers range from 1-112. Items 2 and 4 are *not* counted in the total problem score, but their scores can be entered in the spaces provided at the bottom of the profile. Items 56a-h comprise 8 items. The following 16 items are socially desirable items that are excluded from the problem scores: 6, 15, 28, 49, 59, 60, 73, 78, 80, 88, 92, 98, 106, 107, 108, 109. Comments written by youth at the bottom of page 4 are *not* scored. Place Page 3 scoring template over Page 3 of YSR and Page 4 template over Page 4 of YSR.

Item Scores. If the youth circled 1 or 2 beside an item, enter the 1 or 2 on the appropriate scale of the profile. Note that some items are scored on more than one scale. Problem items that do not belong to any scale are listed under the heading *Other Problems* on the profile. The 16 socially desirable items are *not* listed on the profile. Comments written by the youth should be used in judging whether items deserve to be scored, with the following guidelines:

a. For each problem reported by the youth, only the YSR item that most specifically describes the problem should be scored. If the youth's comments show that more than one item has been scored for a particular problem, or if the youth wrote in a problem for #56h that is specifically covered elsewhere, count only the most specific item.

b. For extreme behaviors (e.g., sets fires, attempts suicide) — if youth noted that it happened once but circled 0 or left it blank, score 1 unless it clearly happened earlier than the 6 months specified in the rating instructions.

c. For items on which youth notes "used to do this," score as the youth scored it, unless it clearly occurred earlier than the 6 months specified in the instructions.

d. When in doubt, score item the way the youth scored it, except on the following items:

Item 9, can't get mind off certain thoughts—this item is *not* restricted to obsessions. It can include almost anything the youth lists here except problems that are specifically listed elsewhere. If the youth wrote "sex" for this item, for example, it would be more appropriately scored on Item 96, *I think about sex too much*. If not covered by another item, responses that might be considered normal for the youth's age should be scored the way the youth scored them; e.g., "cars," "girls," "boys."

Item 40, hears things, & 70, sees things—score experiences such as "ringing in ears" and "spots before eyes" the way the youth scored them; do *not* score experiences while under the influence of drugs or alcohol.

Item 46, nervous movements—if "can't sit still" or anything entirely covered by Item 10 is entered here, score **only** Item 10.

Item 56d, problems with eyes—do *not* score "wear glasses," "near-sighted," and other visual problems having an organic basis.

Item 66, repeats actions—this item is *not* restricted to compulsions. It can include almost anything the youth lists here except problems that are specifically listed elsewhere. Speech repetitions or stammers, for example, would be more appropriately scored on Item 79. *Speech problem.*

Item 77, sleeps more than most—do *not* score "want to stay in bed," but score difficulties in waking up.

Item 84, strange behavior & 85, strange ideas—if what the youth describes is specifically covered by another item, score the more specific item instead.

Item 105, alcohol or drugs—do *not* score tobacco or medication.

SYNDROME SCALE SCORES—To obtain the total raw score for each syndrome scale, sum the 0s, 1s, and 2s you have entered for each scale. Because the items listed under *Other Problems* do not form a scale, a total score is *not* computed for them.

GRAPHIC DISPLAY AND T SCORES

To complete the graphic display for the competence and problem scales, make an X on the number above each scale that equals the total score obtained for that scale. *Be sure to mark the number in the column appropriate for the youth's sex.* Then draw a line to connect the Xs. Percentiles based on nonreferred youths can be read from the left side of the graphic display. *T* scores can be read from the right side.

INTERNALIZING AND EXTERNALIZING—A box at the bottom of the problem profile outlines the computation of Internalizing and Externalizing scores as follows: *Internalizing* = the sum of raw scores for syndrome scales I + II + III, minus the score for Item 103 to avoid counting Item 103 twice, because it is on both Scale I and III. *Externalizing* = the sum of raw scores for syndrome Scales VII + VIII. A *T* score for each Internalizing and Externalizing raw score is listed in the box to the right of the profile. *Be sure to look at the raw score column for the sex of the youth being scored.*

TOTAL PROBLEM SCORE—To compute the total problem score, sum the 1s and 2s on the YSR and enter the sum in the box to the far right of the profile. *Omit Items 2. Allergy, 4. Asthma, and the 16 socially desirable items.* If the youth has entered a problem for Item 56h that is not covered by another item, include the score for 56h. The total problem score can be cross-checked by subtracting the number of problem items scored as present from the sum of 1s and 2s. The difference should equal the number of 2s, omitting Items 2 and 4. (The number and sum of items can *not* be computed by adding scale totals, because some items appear on more than one scale.) A *T* score for each total problem score is listed in the box to the right of the profile. *Be sure to look at the total score column for the sex of the youth being scored.*

SCALE IX. SELF-DESTRUCTIVE/IDENTITY PROBLEMS **FOR BOYS** (**OPTIONAL**)—To obtain the raw scale score for the Self-Destructive/Identity Problems scale, sum the 0s, 1s, and 2s for problem Items *5, 12, 13, 18, 20, 27, 33, 35, 57, 79, 91,* and *110.* Items *12, 18, 33, 35,* and *91* are also scored on the Anxious/Depressed scale. Item *13* is also scored on the Attention Problems scale. Items *20, 27,* and *57* are also scored on the Aggressive Behavior scale. The remaining 3 items are listed under the *Other Problems* heading. The *T* score for each raw score is listed below. The raw score and *T* score can be entered in the box at the bottom of the hand-scored profile.

Raw Score	*T*	Raw Score	*T*
0-1	50	13	79
2	53	14	81
3	58	15	83
4	61	16	85
5	64	17	87
6	66	18	89
7	68	19	91
8	70	20	93
9	72	21	94
10	74	22	96
11	76	23	98
12	78	24	100

APPENDIX B
Mean YSR Scale Scores for Matched Referred and Nonreferred Boys

Scale	T Score				Raw Score				SE of Mean[a]		SE of Meas[b]		Cronbach's alpha
	Referred Mean	SD	Nonreferred Mean	SD	Referred Mean	SD	Nonreferred Mean	SD	Ref	Nonref	Ref	Nonref	
Activities	46.0	8.4	47.8	7.2	4.5	1.6	4.8	1.4	.1	.1	1.3	1.1	.38
Social	43.0	9.6	47.8	7.1	6.2	2.1	7.2	1.8	.1	.1	1.0	.8	.57
Total Competence	44.8	11.7	50.0	9.8	12.9	3.3	14.4	2.7	.2	.1	1.7	1.4	.46
Withdrawn	57.7	8.7	53.8	5.7	4.8	2.7	3.4	2.3	.1	.1	1.7	1.4	.59
Somatic Complaints	58.2	9.3	54.3	6.2	3.6	3.4	2.2	2.3	.1	.1	1.6	1.1	.77
Anxious/Depressed	58.7	9.7	54.2	6.1	8.2	6.1	5.2	4.3	.3	.2	3.2	2.2	.86
Social Problems	58.6	9.3	54.1	5.7	4.1	3.0	2.7	2.1	.1	.1	2.1	1.5	.68
Thought Problems	57.6	9.6	53.8	6.0	3.5	3.0	2.3	2.1	.1	.1	2.2	1.5	.69
Attention Problems	58.6	9.5	54.0	6.0	6.7	3.5	4.7	3.0	.2	.1	2.2	1.8	.75
Delinquent Behavior	59.5	9.2	53.9	6.0	5.4	3.7	3.1	2.5	.2	.1	2.3	1.5	.76
Aggressive Behavior	58.2	9.2	53.9	5.9	11.8	6.9	8.4	5.3	.3	.2	2.9	2.2	.86
Self Dest/Ident Probs	59.2	9.0	54.0	5.9	3.9	3.6	1.9	2.2	.2	.1	2.2	1.3	.76
Internalizing	56.9	11.8	50.1	10.2	16.1	9.9	10.5	7.1	.4	.3	4.9	3.5	.89
Externalizing	56.8	11.6	49.7	9.9	17.3	9.6	11.5	7.1	.4	.3	4.3	3.1	.89
Total Problems	58.0	11.5	50.0	10.1	54.9	26.6	37.3	19.5	1.2	.8	12.4	9.1	.95

Note. N = 536 each in demographically matched referred and nonreferred samples described in Chapter 6. [a]Standard error of mean raw scores. [b]Standard error of measurement = SD $\sqrt{1\text{-reliability}}$ (Guilford, 1965) computed from reliability of raw scores shown in Table 5-1.

APPENDIX B (Continued)

Mean YSR Scale Scores for Matched Referred and Nonreferred Girls

Scale	T Score				Raw Score				SE of Mean[a]		SE of Meas[b]		Cronbach's alpha
	Referred Mean	SD	Nonreferred Mean	SD	Referred Mean	SD	Nonreferred Mean	SD	Ref	Nonref	Ref	Nonref	
Activities	45.4	8.4	48.4	7.0	4.4	1.5	4.9	1.3	.1	.1	.6	.5	.32
Social	42.7	8.7	48.1	7.3	5.9	2.1	7.3	2.1	.1	.1	1.0	.9	.60
Total Competence	43.6	10.6	50.3	10.0	12.6	3.3	14.7	3.0	.2	.1	1.3	1.2	.48
Withdrawn	59.4	8.6	54.1	6.0	5.9	2.7	4.0	2.4	.1	.1	1.3	1.2	.59
Somatic Complaints	58.4	8.5	54.0	5.8	5.0	3.7	3.0	2.9	.2	.1	2.3	1.8	.80
Anxious/Depressed	60.8	10.9	54.2	6.4	11.4	7.2	6.5	5.1	.3	.2	2.6	1.8	.90
Social Problems	58.9	9.2	54.4	6.1	4.2	3.0	2.7	2.2	.1	.1	1.8	1.3	.68
Thought Problems	58.3	9.3	54.2	6.0	3.9	3.1	2.5	2.3	.1	.1	1.8	1.3	.71
Attention Problems	59.8	9.6	54.2	6.1	7.1	3.8	4.7	3.1	.2	.1	1.2	1.0	.78
Delinquent Behavior	61.5	9.2	53.9	5.8	5.4	3.7	2.5	2.2	.2	.1	1.5	.9	.76
Aggressive Behavior	59.9	9.5	54.2	6.1	12.3	6.7	8.1	5.0	.3	.2	3.2	2.4	.86
Internalizing	59.3	11.2	50.4	10.0	21.5	11.1	13.1	8.6	.5	.4	4.2	3.3	.91
Externalizing	59.8	11.8	50.3	10.0	17.7	9.5	10.5	6.4	.4	.3	3.8	2.6	.89
Total Problems	60.5	11.1	50.5	10.2	63.4	28.0	39.6	21.8	1.2	1.0	10.4	8.1	.95

Note. $N = 518$ each in demographically matched referred and nonreferred samples described in Chapter 6. [a]Standard error of mean raw scores. [b]Standard error of measurement = SD $\sqrt{1\text{-reliability}}$ (Guilford, 1965) computed from reliability of raw scores shown in Table 5-1.

APPENDIX C
Pearson Correlations Among YSR T Scores for Boys
Referred Sample above Diagonal, Nonreferred Sample below Diagonal

	Act	Soc	Tot Comp	With-drn	Som	Anx/Dep	Soc Prob	Tht Prob	Att	Del	Agg	Self Dest	Int	Ext	Tot Prob
Activities		.27	.66	-.03	.05	.07	.07	.05	.01	-.12	.05	.03	.05	.00	.04
Social	.23		.81	-.16	.01	-.14	-.16	-.01	-.07	-.07	-.02	-.13	-.14	-.04	-.09
Total Competence	.68	.77		-.12	.05	-.05	-.04	.01	-.07	-.13	.02	-.08	-.07	-.06	-.05
Withdrawn	-.04	.00	-.05		.45	.61	.44	.38	.46	.24	.35	.50	.72	.36	.60
Somatic Complaints	-.03	.01	-.04	.39		.49	.36	.40	.39	.26	.32	.44	.72	.35	.61
Anxious/Depressed	-.03	-.02	-.03	.62	.47		.54	.46	.66	.27	.49	.80	.85	.47	.76
Social Problems	-.11	-.14	-.17	.48	.27	.45		.36	.61	.21	.44	.49	.55	.41	.62
Thought Problems	.02	.05	.05	.31	.25	.35	.26		.45	.36	.45	.45	.50	.45	.61
Attention Problems	-.09	-.09	-.15	.46	.40	.61	.59	.35		.42	.61	.66	.62	.59	.73
Delinquent Behavior	.01	-.04	-.06	.30	.29	.39	.23	.22	.42		.59	.38	.34	.78	.59
Aggressive Behavior	.02	-.01	-.01	.29	.35	.49	.31	.34	.52	.58		.58	.51	.87	.75
Self Dest/Ident Probs	-.02	-.03	-.04	.50	.46	.75	.44	.38	.60	.41	.55		.74	.57	.74
Internalizing	-.01	.02	-.02	.70	.64	.80	.50	.39	.59	.40	.48	.66		.55	.88
Externalizing	.03	.00	-.01	.35	.39	.50	.37	.34	.53	.70	.82	.54	.60		.84
Total Problems	-.01	.02	-.02	.58	.57	.72	.56	.50	.68	.59	.70	.68	.87	.86	

Note. Samples are demographically matched referred and nonreferred youths. $N = 536$ in each sample for problem scales; N ranged from 359 to 439 for competence scales, $rs > .10$ were significant at $p < .05$. $rs > .09$ were significant at $p < .05$; $rs > .09$ were significant at $p < .05$.

APPENDIX C (Continued)
Pearson Correlations Among YSR T Scores for Girls
Referred Sample above Diagonal, Nonreferred Sample below Diagonal

	Act	Soc	Tot Comp	With-drn	Som	Anx/ Dep	Soc Prob	Tht Prob	Att	Del	Agg	Int	Ext	Tot Prob
Activities		.36	.71	-.11	-.05	-.12	-.14	.04	-.16	-.14	-.11	-.11	-.10	-.10
Social	.29		.84	-.24	-.04	-.22	-.25	.04	-.19	-.04	-.05	-.20	-.03	-.14
Total Competence	.65	.82		-.27	-.11	-.28	-.28	.00	-.32	-.15	-.14	-.26	-.15	-.24
Withdrawn	-.10	-.18	-.21		.36	.61	.48	.26	.44	.21	.27	.72	.27	.58
Somatic Complaints	.04	-.09	-.08	.42		.51	.30	.44	.44	.25	.37	.72	.36	.63
Anxious/Depressed	.04	-.10	-.09	.62	.57		.52	.40	.69	.31	.51	.89	.47	.79
Social Problems	-.02	-.12	-.14	.49	.33	.47		.30	.54	.17	.42	.53	.37	.60
Thought Problems	.05	.01	-.02	.29	.35	.50	.28		.47	.32	.49	.47	.46	.62
Attention Problems	-.04	-.11	-.17	.41	.46	.63	.53	.46		.44	.60	.66	.59	.78
Delinquent Behavior	-.02	-.10	-.09	.29	.34	.45	.18	.35	.43		.62	.33	.81	.59
Aggressive Behavior	.03	-.05	-.05	.30	.43	.56	.38	.48	.59	.50		.51	.90	.78
Internalizing	.03	-.12	-.12	.69	.72	.81	.53	.49	.60	.44	.55		.50	.87
Externalizing	.01	-.06	-.06	.38	.46	.57	.39	.49	.58	.67	.82	.67		.81
Total Problems	.02	-.10	-.11	.59	.64	.76	.57	.61	.70	.56	.72	.91	.86	

Note. Samples are demographically matched referred and nonreferred youths. $N = 518$ in each sample for problem scales; N ranged from 355 to 440 for competence scales, $rs > .10$ were significant at $p < .05$. $rs > .09$ were significant at $p < .05$.

Algina, J., 19, 21, 206
Abramowitz, M., 21, 205
Abuse, 179
Academic performance, 14, 23, 86
Accountability for services, 157
Achenbach, T.M., 1, 3-5, 14-17, 25, 27, 31-34, 38, 47, 52, 56, 58, 62-65, 73, 80, 86, 96, 118, 124, 130, 144, 155, 163, 170-174, 180-191, 194, 205-207
Activities scale, 14, 18, 66, 68
Age differences, 56, 68, 90, 118
Aggressive Behavior, 39, 40, 47, 49
Allergy, 8, 38, 63
American Psychiatric Association, 65, 154, 206
Anxious/Depressed, 36, 47, 48, 68, 72
Assessment, 172
Asthma, 8, 38, 63
Attention Problems, 49, 72
Barrett, C.L., 58, 208
Beall, G., 57, 208
Bennett, B., 125, 208
Bernstein, G.A., 125, 206
Bird, H.R., 118, 170, 182, 186, 189, 205
Borderline clinical range, 22, 23, 43-45, 72
Brown, J.S., 131, 164, 180, 182, 205
Canino, G.J., 118, 170, 205
Caputo, J., 58, 207
Case registers, 159, 171-172
Child Behavior Checklist for Ages 4-18 (CBCL/4-18), 5, 56, 65, 145-150, 155, 182
Clinical range, 23, 43-45
Clinical interviews, 4, 133-134
Clinical interpretations, 130, 203
Cognitive, 4, 194

Cohen, B.H., 57, 208
Cohen, J., 66, 68, 84, 118, 206, 208
Compas, B.E., 59
Competence, 5, 14-24, 66, 83-90
Computer scoring, 23, 34, 43
Confidentiality, 133, 150-151
Conover, N.C., 56, 207
Content validity, 63
Core syndromes, 30-32
Costello, A.J., 56, 65, 155, 206
Criterion related validity, 65-68
Crocker, L., 19, 21, 206
Cronbach, L.J., 60, 206
Cronbach's alpha, 60
Cross-informant correlations, 187-189
Cross-informant syndromes, 32-35
Cross-cultural, 170, 182-183
Cross-informant computer program, 34
Cutpoints, 44-45, 72, 173
de Jong, J.B., 208
Delinquent Behavior, 47, 49, 68, 79, 201
Demographic differences, 68, 86, 97, 118
Diagnosis, 154-155, 172-174, 178
Diagnostic Interview Schedule for Children (DISC), 56, 173
Diagnostic and Statistical Manual (DSM), 65, 160, 154-55, 173
Direct Observation Form (DOF), 4, 137, 145-150
Dulcan, M.K., 56, 206
Edelbrock, C., 1, 14, 17, 25, 27, 31, 47, 56, 58, 63, 65, 86, 118, 124, 155, 170, 205, 206
Educable Mentally Retarded (EMR), 144
Education of the Handicapped Act, 17, 144-147, 207

Epidemiology, 169-172
Ethnicity, 16, 64, 68, 72, 202
Etiology, 174-175
Evans, W.R., 58, 207
Externalizing, 47-53, 68, 118
Factor analyses, 25, 48
False positives, 45, 76, 77, 79
False negatives, 45, 76, 77, 78
Farley, G.K., 64, 86, 209
Finch, A.J., 125, 208
Fleiss, J.L., 73, 207
Forensic, 153
French, N.H., 64, 207
Garfinkel, D.B., 125, 206
Gent, C.L., 52, 207
Gorsuch, R.L., 26, 48, 207
Gould, M., 118, 170, 205
Grayson, D., 118, 206
Greenbaum, R., 207
Grimes, K., 65, 155, 208
Guilford, J.P., 207, 215-216
Hampe, E., 58, 208
Hand-scored profile, 23, 34, 43
Handicapped, 145, 194
Harter, S., 86, 207
Hensley, V.R., 118, 187, 206
Hersen, M., 125, 208
Hollingshead, A.B., 27, 64, 65, 83, 207
Howell, D.C., 57
Intake, 132, 160
Internal consistency, 59-60
Internalizing, 47-53, 68, 118
Interventions, 134-137, 142-144, 177-178
IQ, 51
Kalas, R., 56, 206
Katz, R.S., 52, 207
Kazdin, A.E., 64, 125, 207, 208
Kessler, M.D., 65, 155, 206
Köferl, P., 170, 182, 187, 207
Last, C.G., 125, 208
Learning Disabled (LD), 144

Lewis, M., 52, 206
Lie scale, 203
Loney, J., 58, 207
Low scores, 202
Mabe, P.A., 125, 208
Machine-readable form, 196
McConaughy, S.H., 16, 52, 144, 194, 206, 207
Medical, 151-152, 180-181
Mental health services, 65, 132-144
Milich, R., 58, 207
Miller, L.C., 47, 58, 207, 208
Mish, F.C., 201
Multiaxial assessment, 2, 3
Needs assessment, 157
Noam, G.G., 65, 155, 208
Noble, H., 58, 208
Norms, 16, 17, 19, 24, 38, 41, 166-168, 194
Odds ratios, 73-76
Other Problems, 36, 201
Outcome, 143, 176-177
Pediatric psychologists, 151
Perceived Competence Scale for Children, 86
Percentiles, 18, 39
Peterson, D.R., 47, 208
Phares, V.S., 57, 118, 170, 205, 206
Pickett, R.M., 45, 208
Piers, E.V., 64, 208
Planning, 155
Population studies, 170
Pre-1991 scales, 122-128
Prince, F., 170, 208
Principal components analyses, 25, 27, 28, 48
Problem items, 8, 66, 90-120
Public Law 94-142, 17, 144, 154
Rating intervals, 11, 195
Raw scores, 39, 165-167
Reading skills, 12, 16, 193, 194
Referral status, 66, 84, 91

Relative Operating Characteristics (ROC), 45
Reliability, 55-58
Remschmidt, H., 170, 182, 187, 208
Research, 163-184
Risk factors, 177
Roberts, M., 58, 207
Robins, L.N., 58, 208
Rubio-Stipec, M., 118, 170, 205
Sakoda, A., 57, 66, 84, 91, 97, 208
SAS Institute, 78, 208
Sawyer, M.G., 182, 186, 189, 208
Saylor, C.F., 125, 208
School psychologist, 148-151
School, 144
Scoring templates, 200, 212
Self-Destructive/Identity Problems, 26, 31, 36, 79
Severely Emotionally Disturbed (SED), 145-150
Sex differences, 118, 202
Short form, 196
Snook, S.C., 48
Social Scale, 14, 18, 72, 84
Social desirability, 193
Social Problems, 49, 66, 79, 187
Socially desirable items, 119-120
Socioeconomic status (SES), 16, 27, 64, 68, 72, 90, 97
Somatic Complaints, 29, 47, 48, 68, 79
Special education, 144
Spirito, A., 125, 208
Stability, 58-59
Stanger, C., 16, 207
Stegun, I.A., 21, 205
Stone, K., 65, 155, 208
Strauss, C.C., 125, 208
Swets, J.E., 45, 208
Syndrome, 25-46
T scores, 18, 38-45, 165-167
Taxonomy, 25, 172

Teacher's Report Form (TRF), 56, 65, 145-150, 155, 182
Thought Problems, 39, 49
Total Competence score, 23, 72, 76, 78, 86, 199
Total Problem score, 41, 45, 68, 68, 72, 76, 78, 199
Training, 159-161
Translations, 182, 193
Treiber, F.A., 125, 208
Unanswered items, 199
Unhappy, sad, or depressed, 38, 80, 91
Unis, A.S., 64, 207
Validity, 62-81
van der Ende, J., 189, 208
Verhulst, F.C., 170, 182, 187, 189, 208
Vervuurt-Poot, C., 170, 208
Walter, B.R., 170, 182, 187, 208
Wechsler, D., 51, 208
Weinstein, S.R., 65, 155, 173, 208
Weintraub, S.A., 52, 209
Williams, R., 57
Withdrawn, 34, 47, 48, 68, 72, 79
Young Adult Self-Report (YASR), 189
Young Adult Behavior Checklist (YABCL), 189
Zalk, S.R., 52, 207
Zigler, E., 52, 207
Zimet, S.G., 64, 86, 209